Don C
2280
Memphis, TN.
U.S.A.

THE KNOWLEDGE OF THE HOLY

God looks Dow To All Who Look Up!

5 June NOV. 1988.

By the same author:

BEST OF A. W. TOZER
BORN AFTER MIDNIGHT
CHRIST THE ETERNAL SON
THE DIVINE CONQUEST
ECHOES FROM EDEN
FAITH BEYOND REASON
GOD TELLS THE MAN WHO CARES
HOW TO BE FILLED WITH THE HOLY SPIRIT
I CALL IT HERESY
I TALK BACK TO THE DEVIL
JESUS, OUR MAN IN GLORY
LEANING INTO THE WIND
LET MY PEOPLE GO
MAN: THE DWELLING PLACE OF GOD
MEN WHO MET GOD
THE NEXT CHAPTER AFTER THE LAST
OF GOD AND MEN
PATHS TO POWER
RENEWED DAY BY DAY
THE PURSUIT OF GOD
THE ROOT OF THE RIGHTEOUS
THE SET OF THE SAIL
THAT INCREDIBLE CHRISTIAN
TRAGEDY IN THE CHURCH
WHATEVER HAPPENED TO WORSHIP?
WHEN HE IS COME
WHO PUT JESUS ON THE CROSS?
WORSHIP: THE MISSING JEWEL

THE KNOWLEDGE OF THE HOLY

A. W. TOZER

STL Books
Bromley, Kent
Kingsway Publications
Eastbourne

First STL edition 1976
Reprinted 1977, 1981 1984
This edition 1987

Published by arrangement with James Clarke & Co. Ltd.

British Library Cataloguing in Publication Data

Tozer, A. W.
The Knowledge of the Holy.
1. God
I. Title
231 BT102

STL ISBN 1 85078 031 5
Kingsway ISBN 0 86065 592 X

STL Books are published by Send The Light (Operation Mobilisation), PO Box 48, Bromley, Kent, England.

Published jointly with Kingsway Publications Ltd, Lottbridge Drove, Eastbourne, E. Sussex, BN23 6NT

Cover photo: Tony Stone Associates Ltd.

Typesetting, production and printing in England by Nuprint Ltd, Harpenden, Herts, AL5 4SE.

Contents

Author's Introduction

True religion confronts earth with heaven and brings eternity to bear upon time. The messenger of Christ, though he speaks from God, must also, as the Quakers used to say, 'speak to the condition' of his hearers; otherwise he will speak a language known only to himself. His message must be not only timeless but timely. He must speak to his own generation.

The message of this book does not grow out of these times but it is appropriate to them. It is called forth by a condition which has existed in the Church for some years and is steadily growing worse. I refer to the loss of the concept of majesty from the popular religious mind. The Church has surrendered her once lofty concept of God and has substituted for it one so low, so ignoble, as to be utterly unworthy of thinking, worshipping men. This she has done not deliberately, but little by little and without her knowledge; and her very unawareness only makes her situation all the more tragic.

The low view of God entertained almost universally among Christians is the cause of a hundred lesser evils everywhere among us. A whole new philosophy of the Christian life has resulted from this one basic error in our religious thinking.

With our loss of the sense of majesty has come the

further loss of religious awe and consciousness of the divine presence. We have lost our spirit of worship and our ability to withdraw inwardly to meet God in adoring silence. Modern Christianity is simply not producing the kind of Christian who can appreciate or experience the life in the Spirit. The words, 'Be still, and know that I am God,'[1] mean next to nothing to the self-confident, bustling worshipper in this middle period of the twentieth century.

This loss of the concept of majesty has come just when the forces of religion are making dramatic gains and the churches are more prosperous than at any time within the past several hundred years. But the alarming thing is that our gains are mostly external and our losses wholly internal; and since it is the *quality* of our religion that is affected by internal conditions, it may be that our supposed gains are but losses spread over a wider field.

The only way to recoup our spiritual losses is to go back to the cause of them and make such corrections as the truth warrants. The decline of the knowledge of the holy has brought on our troubles. A rediscovery of the majesty of God will go a long way toward curing them. It is impossible to keep our moral practices sound and our inward attitudes right while our idea of God is erroneous or inadequate. If we would bring back spiritual power to our lives, we must begin to think of God more nearly as He is.

As my humble contribution to a better understanding of the majesty of the heavens I offer this reverent study of the attributes of God. Were Christians today reading such works as those of Augustine or Anselm a book like this would have no reason for being. But such illuminated masters are known to modern Christians only by name. Publishers dutifully reprint their books and in due time these appear on the shelves of our studies. But the whole trouble lies right there: they remain on the shelves. The current religious mood makes the reading of them virtually impossible even for educated Christians.

Apparently not many Christians will wade through hundreds of pages of heavy religious matter requiring sustained concentration. Such books remind too many persons of the secular classics they were forced to read while they were in school and they turn away from them with a feeling of discouragement.

For that reason an effort such as this may be not without some beneficial effect. Since this book is neither esoteric nor technical, and since it is written in the language of worship with no pretension to elegant literary style, perhaps some persons may be drawn to read it. While I believe that nothing will be found here contrary to sound Christian theology, I yet write not for professional theologians but for plain persons whose hearts stir them up to seek after God Himself.

It is my hope that this small book may contribute somewhat to the promotion of personal heart religion among us; and should a few persons by reading it be encouraged to begin the practice of reverent meditation on the being of God, that will more than repay the labour required to produce it.

Notes

1 Ps. 46:10.

1

Why We Must Think Rightly About God

O Lord God Almighty, not the God of the philosophers and the wise but the God of the prophets and apostles; and better than all, the God and Father of our Lord Jesus Christ, may I express Thee unblamed?

They that know Thee not may call upon Thee as other than Thou art, and so worship not Thee but a creature of their own fancy; therefore enlighten our minds that we may know Thee as Thou art, so that we may perfectly love Thee and worthily praise Thee.

In the name of Jesus Christ our Lord. Amen.

What comes into our minds when we think about God is the most important thing about us.

The history of mankind will probably show that no people has ever risen above its religion, and man's spiritual history will positively demonstrate that no religion has ever been greater than its idea of God. Worship is pure or base as the worshipper entertains high or low thoughts of God.

For this reason the gravest question before the Church is always God Himself, and the most portentous fact about any man is not what he at a given time may say or do, but what he in his deep heart conceives God to be like. We tend by a secret law of the soul to move toward our mental image of God. This is true not only of the individual

Christian, but of the company of Christians that composes the Church. Always the most revealing thing about the Church is her idea of God, just as her most significant message is what she says about Him or leaves unsaid, for her silence is often more eloquent than her speech. She can never escape the self-disclosure of her witness concerning God.

Were we able to extract from any man a complete answer to the question, 'What comes into your mind when you think about God?' we might predict with certainty the spiritual future of that man. Were we able to know exactly what our most influential religious leaders think of God today, we might be able with some precision to foretell where the Church will stand tomorrow.

Without doubt, the mightiest thought the mind can entertain is the thought of God, and the weightiest word in any language is its word for God. Thought and speech are God's gifts to creatures made in His image; these are intimately associated with Him and impossible apart from Him. It is highly significant that the first word was the Word.

> And the Word was with God, and the Word was God.[1]

We may speak because God spoke. In Him word and idea are indivisible.

That our idea of God correspond as nearly as possible to the true being of God is of immense importance to us. Compared with our actual thoughts about Him, our creedal statements are of little consequence. Our real idea of God may lie buried under the rubbish of conventional religious notions and may require an intelligent and vigorous search before it is finally unearthed and exposed for what it is. Only after an ordeal of painful self-probing are we likely to discover what we actually believe about God.

A right conception of God is basic not only to systematic theology but to practical Christian living as well. It is to worship what the foundation is to the temple; where it is inadequate or out of plumb the whole structure must sooner or later collapse. I believe there is scarcely an error in doctrine or a failure in applying Christian ethics that cannot be traced finally to imperfect and ignoble thoughts about God.

It is my opinion that the Christian conception of God current in these middle years of the twentieth century is so decadent as to be utterly beneath the dignity of the Most High God and actually to constitute for professed believers something amounting to a moral calamity.

All the problems of heaven and earth, though they were to confront us together and at once, would be nothing compared with the overwhelming problem of God: That He *is*, what He is *like*; and what we as moral beings must *do* about Him.

The man who comes to a right belief about God is relieved of ten thousand temporal problems, for he sees at once that these have to do with matters which at the most cannot concern him for very long; but even if the multiple burdens of time may be lifted from him, the one mighty single burden of eternity begins to press down upon him with a weight more crushing than all the woes of the world piled one upon another. That mighty burden is his obligation to God. It includes an instant and lifelong duty to love God with every power of mind and soul, to obey Him perfectly, and to worship Him acceptably. And when the man's labouring conscience tells him that he has done none of these things, but has from childhood been guilty of foul revolt against the Majesty in the heavens, the inner pressure of self-accusation may become too heavy to bear.

The gospel can lift this destroying burden from the mind, give beauty for ashes, and the garment of praise for the spirit of heaviness. But unless the weight of the burden is felt the gospel can mean nothing to the man; and until he sees a vision of God high and lifted up, there will be no woe and no burden. Low views of God destroy the gospel for all who hold them.

Among the sins to which the human heart is prone, hardly any other is more hateful to God than idolatry, for idolatry is at bottom a libel on His character. The idolatrous heart assumes that God is other than He is – in itself a monstrous sin – and substitutes for the true God one made after its own likeness. Always this God will conform to the image of the one who created it and will be base or pure, cruel or kind, according to the moral state of the mind from which it emerges.

A god begotten in the shadows of a fallen heart will quite naturally be no true likeness of the true God. 'Thou thoughtest,' said the Lord to the wicked man in the psalm, 'that I was altogether such an one as thyself.'[2] Surely this must be a serious affront to the Most High God before whom cherubim and seraphim continually do cry, 'Holy, holy, holy, Lord God of Sabaoth.'

Let us beware lest we in our pride accept the erroneous notion that idolatry consists only in kneeling before visible objects of adoration, and that civilised peoples are therefore free from it. The essence of idolatry is the entertainment of thoughts about God that are unworthy of Him. It begins in the mind and may be present where no overt act of worship has taken place. 'When they knew God,' wrote Paul, 'they glorified him not as God, neither were thankful; but became vain in their imagination, and their foolish heart was darkened.'[3]

Then followed the worship of idols fashioned after the likeness of men and birds and beasts and creeping things. But this series of degrading acts began in the mind. Wrong ideas about God are not only the fountain from which the polluted waters of idolatry flow; they are themselves idolatrous. The idolater simply imagines things about

God and acts as if they were true.

Perverted notions about God soon rot the religion in which they appear. The long career of Israel demonstrates this clearly enough, and the history of the Church confirms it. So necessary to the Church is a lofty concept of God that when that concept in any measure declines, the Church with her worship and her moral standards declines along with it. The first step down for any church is taken when it surrenders its high opinion of God.

Before the Christian Church goes into eclipse anywhere there must first be a corrupting of her simple basic theology. She simply gets a wrong answer to the question, 'What is God like?' and goes on from there. Though she may continue to cling to a sound nominal creed, her practical working creed has become false. The masses of her adherents come to believe that God is different from what He actually is; and that is heresy of the most insidious and deadly kind.

The heaviest obligation lying upon the Christian Church today is to purify and elevate her concept of God until it is once more worthy of Him – and of her. In all her prayers and labours this should have first place. We do the greatest service to the next generation of Christians by passing on to them undimmed and undiminished that noble concept of God which we received from our Hebrew and Christian fathers of generations past. This will prove of greater value to them than anything that art or science can devise.

> O God of Bethel, by whose hand
> Thy people still are fed;
> Who through this weary pilgrimage
> Hast all our fathers led!

Our vows, our prayers we now present
  Before Thy throne of grace:
God of our fathers! be the God
  Of their succeeding race.

Philip Doddridge

Notes

1 John 1:1.
2 Ps. 50:21.
3 Rom. 1:21.

2

God Incomprehensible

Lord, how great is our dilemma! In Thy presence silence best becomes us, but love inflames our hearts and constrains us to speak.

Were we to hold our peace the stones would cry out; yet if we speak, what shall we say? Teach us to know that we cannot know, for the things of God knoweth no man, but the Spirit of God. Let faith support us where reason fails, and we shall think because we believe, not in order that we may believe.

In Jesus' name. Amen.

The child, the philosopher, and the religionist have all one question: 'What is God like?'

This book is an attempt to answer that question. Yet at the outset I must acknowledge that it cannot be answered except to say that God is not like anything; that is, He is not *exactly* like anything or anybody.

We learn by using what we already know as a bridge over which we pass to the unknown. It is not possible for the mind to crash suddenly past the familiar into the totally unfamiliar. Even the most vigorous and daring mind is unable to create something out of nothing by a spontaneous act of imagination. Those strange beings that populate the world of mythology and superstition are not pure creations of fancy. The imagination created them by taking the ordinary inhabitants of earth and air and sea and extending their familiar forms beyond their normal boundaries, or by mixing the forms of two or more so as to produce something new. However beautiful or grotesque these may be, their prototypes can always be identified. They are like something we already know.

The effort of inspired men to express the ineffable has placed a great strain upon both thought and language in the Holy Scriptures. These being often a revelation of a world *above* nature, and the minds for which they were written being a *part* of nature, the writers are compelled to use a great many 'like' words to make themselves understood.

When the Spirit would acquaint us with something that lies beyond the field of our knowledge, He tells us that *this* thing is *like* something we already know, but He is always careful to phrase His description so as to save us from slavish literalism. For example, when the prophet Ezekiel saw heaven opened and beheld visions of God, he found himself looking at that which he had no language to describe. What he was seeing was wholly different from anything he had ever known before, so he fell back upon the language of resemblance.

> As for the likeness of the living creatures, their appeareance was like burning coals of fire.[1]

The nearer he approaches to the burning throne the less sure his words become:

> And above the firmament that was over their heads was the likeness of a throne, as the appearance of a sapphire stone: and upon the likeness of the throne was the likeness as the appearance of a man above upon it. And I saw as the colour of amber, as the appearance of fire round about within it.... This was the appearance of the likeness of the glory of the Lord.[2]

Strange as this language is, it still does not create the impression of unreality. One gathers that the whole scene is very real but entirely alien to anything men know on earth. So, in order to convey an idea of what he sees, the prophet must employ such words as 'likeness', 'appearance', 'as it were', and 'the likeness of the appearance'. Even the throne becomes 'the appearance of a throne' and He that sits upon it, though like a man, is so *unlike* one that He can be described only as 'the likeness of the appearance of a man'.

When the Scripture states that man was made in the image of God, we dare not add to that statement an idea from our own head and make it mean 'in the *exact* image'. To do so is to make man a replica of God, and that is to lose the unicity of God and end with no God at all. It is to break down the wall, infinitely high, that separates that-which-is-God from that-which-is-not-God. To think of creature and Creator as alike in essential being is to rob God of most of His attributes and reduce Him to the status of a creature. It is, for instance, to rob Him of His infinitude: there cannot be two unlimited substances in the universe. It is to take away His sovereignty: there cannot be two absolutely free beings in the universe, for sooner or later two completely free wills must collide. These attributes, to mention no more, require that there be but one to whom they belong.

When we try to imagine what God is like we must of necessity use that-which-is-not-God as the raw material for our minds to work on; hence whatever we visualise God to be, He is not, for we have constructed our image out of that which He has made and what He has made is not God. If we insist upon trying to imagine Him, we end with an idol, made not with hands but with thoughts; and an idol of the mind is as offensive to God as an idol of the hand.

'The intellect knoweth that it is ignorant of Thee,' said

Nicholas of Cusa, 'because it knoweth Thou canst not be known, unless the unknowable could be known, and the invisible beheld, and the inaccessible attained.'[3]

'If anyone should set forth any concept by which Thou canst be conceived,' says Nicholas again, 'I know that that concept is not a concept of Thee, for every concept is ended in the wall of Paradise.... So too, if any were to tell of the understanding of Thee, wishing to supply a means whereby Thou mightest be understood, this man is yet far from Thee...forasmuch as Thou art absolute above all the concepts which any man can frame.'[4]

Left to ourselves we tend immediately to reduce God to manageable terms. We want to get Him where we can use Him, or at least know where He is when we need Him. We want a God we can in some measure control. We need the feeling of security that comes from knowing what God is like, and what He is like is of course a composite of all the religious pictures we have seen, all the best people we have known or heard about, and all the sublime ideas we have entertained.

If all this sounds strange to modern ears, it is only because we have for a full half century taken God for granted. The glory of God has not been revealed to this generation of men. The God of contemporary Christianity is only slightly superior to the gods of Greece and Rome, if indeed He is not actually inferior to them in that He is weak and helpless while they at least had power.

If what we conceive God to be He is not, how then shall we think of Him? If He is indeed incomprehensible, as the Creed declares Him to be, and unapproachable, as Paul says He is, how can we Christians satisfy our longing after Him? The hopeful words, 'Acquaint now thyself with him, and be at peace',[5] still stand after the passing of the centuries; but how shall we acquaint ourselves with One who eludes all the straining efforts of mind and heart? And how shall we be held accountable to know what cannot be known?

'Canst thou by searching find out God?' asks Zophar the Naamathite; 'canst thou find out the Almighty unto perfection? It is as high as heaven; what canst thou do? deeper than hell; what canst thou know?'[6] 'Neither knoweth any man the Father, save the Son,' said our Lord, 'and he to whomsoever the Son will reveal him.'[7] The *Gospel According to John* reveals the helplessness of the human mind before the great Mystery which is God, and Paul in 1 Corinthians teaches that God can be known only as the Holy Spirit performs in the seeking heart an act of self-disclosure.

The yearning to know what cannot be known, to comprehend the incomprehensible, to touch and taste the unapproachable, arises from the image of God in the nature of man. Deep calleth unto deep, and though polluted and landlocked by the mighty disaster theologians call the Fall, the soul senses its origin and longs to return to its source. How can this be realised?

The answer of the Bible is simply 'through Jesus Christ our Lord'. In Christ and by Christ, God effects complete self-disclosure, although He shows Himself not to reason but to faith and love. Faith is an organ of knowledge, and love an organ of experience. God came to us in the incarnation; in atonement He reconciled us to Himself, and by faith and love we enter and lay hold on Him.

'Verily God is of infinite greatness,' says Christ's enraptured troubadour, Richard Rolle; 'more than we can think;... unknowable by created things; and can never be comprehended by us as He is in Himself. But even here and now, whenever the heart begins to burn with a desire for God, she is made able to receive the uncreated light and, inspired and fulfilled by the gifts of the Holy Ghost, she tastes the joys of heaven. She transcends all visible things and is raised to the sweetness of eternal life.... Herein truly is perfect love; when all the intent of the mind, all the secret working of the heart, is lifted up into the love of God.'[8]

That God can be known by the soul in tender personal experience while remaining infinitely aloof from the curious eyes of reason constitutes a paradox best described as

> Darkness to the intellect
> But sunshine to the heart.
> *Frederick W. Faber*

The author of the celebrated little work *The Cloud of Unknowing* develops this thesis throughout his book. In appoaching God, he says, the seeker discovers that the divine being dwells in obscurity, hidden behind a cloud of unknowing; nevertheless he should not be discouraged but set his will with a naked intent unto God. This cloud is between the seeker and God so that he may never see God clearly by the light of understanding nor feel Him in the emotions. But by the mercy of God faith can break through into His presence if the seeker but believe the Word and press on.[9]

Michael de Molinos, the Spanish saint, taught the same thing. In his *Spiritual Guide* he says that God will take the soul by the hand and lead her through the way of pure faith, 'and causing the understanding to leave behind all considerations and reasonings He draws her forward.... Thus He causes her by means of a simple and obscure knowledge of faith to aspire only to her Bridegroom upon the wings of love.'[10]

For these and similar teachings Molinos was condemned as a heretic by the Inquisition and sentenced to life imprisonment. He soon died in prison, but the truth he taught can never die. Speaking of the Christian soul he says: 'Let her suppose that all the whole world and the most refined conceptions of the wisest intellects can tell her nothing, and that the goodness and beauty of her Beloved infinitely surpass all their knowledge, being persuaded that all creatures are too rude to inform her and to conduct her to the true knowledge of God.... She ought then to go forward with her love, leaving all her understanding behind. Let her love God as He is in Himself, and not as her imagination says He is, and pictures Him.'[11]

'What is God like?' If by that question we mean 'What is God like *in Himself*?' there is no answer. If we mean 'What has God disclosed *about Himself* that the reverent reason can comprehend?' there is, I believe, an answer both full and satisfying. For while the name of God is secret and His essential nature incomprehensible, He in condescending love has by revelation declared certain things to be true of Himself. These we call His attributes.

> Sovereign Father, heavenly King,
> Thee we now presume to sing;
> Glad Thine attributes confess,
> Glorious all, and numberless.
>
> *Charles Wesley*

Notes

1 Ezek. 1:13.
2 Ezek. 1:26–28.
3 Nicholas of Cusa, *The Vision of God* (E. P. Dutton & Sons, New York, 1928) p.60.
4 *Ibid* pp.58–59.
5 Job 22:21.
6 Job 11:7–8.
7 Matt. 11:27.
8 Richard Rolle, *The Amending of Life* (John M. Watkins, London, 1922) pp.83–84.
9 *The Cloud of Unknowing* (John M. Watkins, London 1946).
10 Michael de Molinos, *The Spiritual Guide* (Methune & Co, Ltd), London, sixth edition, 1950) p.56.
11 *Ibid* pp.56–57.

3

A Divine Attribute: Something True About God

O Majesty unspeakable, my soul desires to behold Thee. I cry to Thee from the dust.

Yet when I inquire after Thy name it is secret. Thou art hidden in the light which no man can approach unto. What Thou art cannot be thought or uttered, for Thy glory is ineffable.

Still, prophet and psalmist, apostle and saint have encouraged me to believe that I may in some measure know Thee. Therefore, I pray, whatever of Thyself Thou hast been pleased to disclose, help me to search out as treasure more precious than rubies or the merchandise of fine gold: for with Thee shall I live when the stars of the twilight are no more and the heavens have vanished away and only Thou remainest. Amen.

The study of the attributes of God, far from being dull and heavy, may for the enlightened Christian be a sweet and absorbing spiritual exercise. To the soul that is athirst for God, nothing could be more delightful.

Only to sit and think of God,
Oh what a joy it is!
To think the thought, to breathe the name
Earth has no higher bliss.

Frederick W. Faber

It would seem to be necessary before proceeding further to define the word *attribute* as it is used in this volume. It is not used in its philosophical sense nor confined to its strictest theological meaning. By it is meant simply whatever may be correctly ascribed to God. For the purpose of this book *an attribute of God is whatever God has in any way revealed as being true of Himself.*

And this brings us to the question of the number of the divine attributes. Religious thinkers have differed about this. Some have insisted that there are seven, but Faber sang of the 'God of a *thousand* attributes,' and Charles Wesley exclaimed,

> Glad thine attributes confess,
> Glorious all and *numberless*.

True, these men were worshipping, not counting; but we might be wise to follow the insight of the enraptured heart rather than the more cautious reasonings of the theological mind. If an attribute is something that is true of God, we may as well not try to enumerate them. Furthermore, to this meditation on the being of God the number of the attributes is not important, for only a limited few will be mentioned here.

If an attribute is something true of God, it is also something that we can *conceive* as being true of Him. God, being infinite, must possess attributes about which we can know nothing. An attribute, as we can know it, is a mental concept, an intellectual response to God's self-revelation. It is an answer to a question, the reply God makes to our interrogation concerning Himself.

What is God like? What kind of God is He? How may we expect Him to act toward us and toward all created things? Such questions are not merely academic. They touch the far-in reaches of the human spirit, and their answers affect life and character and destiny. When asked in reverence and their answers sought in humility; these are questions that cannot but be pleasing to our Father which art in heaven. 'For He willeth that we be occupied in knowing and loving,' wrote Julian of Norwich, 'till the time that we shall be fulfilled in heaven. . . . For of all things the beholding and the loving of the Maker maketh the soul to seem less in his own sight, and most filleth him with reverent dread and true meekness; with plenty of charity for his fellow Christians.'[1]

To our questions God has provided answers; not all the answers, certainly, but enough to satisfy our intellects and ravish our hearts. These answers He has provided in nature, in the Scriptures, and in the person of His Son.

The idea that God reveals Himself in the creation is not held with much vigour by modern Christians; but it is, nevertheless, set forth in the inspired Word, especially in the writings of David and Isaiah in the Old Testament and in Paul's *Epistle to the Romans* in the New. In the Holy Scriptures the revelation is clearer.

> The heavens declare Thy glory, Lord,
> In every star Thy wisdom shines;
> But when our eyes behold Thy Word,
> We read Thy name in fairer lines.
>
> *Isaac Watts*

And it is a sacred and indispensable part of the Christian message that the full sun-blaze of revelation came at the incarnation when the Eternal Word became flesh to dwell among us.

Though God in this threefold revelation has provided answers to our questions concerning Him, the answers by no means lie on the surface. They must be sought by prayer, by long meditation on the written Word, and by earnest and well-disciplined labour. However brightly the light may shine, it can be seen only by those who are spiritually prepared to receive it.

> Blessed are the pure in heart: for they shall see God.[2]

If we would think accurately about the attributes of God, we must learn to reject certain words that are sure to come crowding into our minds – such words as *trait, characteristic, quality,* words which are proper and necessary when we are considering created beings but altogether inappropriate when we are thinking about God. We must break ourselves of the habit of thinking of the Creator as we think of His creatures. It is probably impossible to think without words, but if we permit ourselves to think with the wrong words, we shall soon be entertaining erroneous thoughts; for words, which are given us for the expression of thought, have a habit of going beyond their proper bounds and determining the content of thought. 'As nothing is more easy than to think,' says Thomas Traherne, 'so nothing is more difficult than to think well.'[3] If we ever think well it should be when we think of God.

A man is the sum of his parts and his character the sum of the traits that compose it. These traits vary from man to man and may from time to time vary from themselves within the same man. Human character is not constant because the traits or qualities that constitute it are unstable. These come and go, burn low or glow with great intensity throughout our lives. Thus a man who is kind and considerate at thirty may be cruel and churlish at fifty. Such a change is possible because man is *made*; he is in a very real sense a composition; he is the sum of the traits that make up his character.

We naturally and correctly think of man as a work wrought by the divine Intelligence. He is both created and made. How he was created lies undisclosed among the secrets of God; how he was brought from not-being to being, from no-thing to some-thing is not known and may never be known to any but the One who brought him forth. How God *made* him, however, is less of a secret, and while we know only a small portion of the whole truth, we do know that man possesses a body, a soul, and a spirit; we know that he has memory, reason, will, intelligence, sensation, and we know that to give these meaning he has the wondrous gift of consciousness. We know, too, that these, together with various qualities of temperament, compose his total human self. These are gifts from God arranged by infinite wisdom, notes that make up the score of creation's loftiest symphony, threads that compose the master tapestry of the universe.

But in all this we are thinking creature-thoughts and using creature-words to express them. Neither such thoughts nor such words are appropriate to the Deity. 'The Father is made of none,' says the Athanasian Creed, 'neither created nor begotten. The Son is of the Father alone, not made, nor created, but begotten. The Holy Spirit is of the Father and the Son: not made nor created, nor begotten, but proceeding.'[4] God exists in Himself and of Himself. His being He owes to no one. His substance is indivisible. He has no parts but is single in His unitary being.

The doctrine of the divine unity means not only that there is but one God; it means also that God is simple, uncomplex, one with Himself. The harmony of His being is the result not of a perfect balance of parts but of the absence of parts. Between His attributes no contradiction can exist. He need not suspend one to exercise another, for in Him all His attributes are one. All of God does all that God does; He does not divide Himself to perform a work, but works in the total unity of His being.

An attribute, then, is not a part of God. It is *how* God is, and as far as the reasoning mind can go, we may say that it is *what* God is, though, as I have tried to explain, exactly what He is He cannot tell us. Of what God is conscious when He is conscious of self, only He knows.

> The things of God knoweth no man, but the Spirit of God.[5]

Only to an equal could God communicate the mystery of His Godhead; and to think of God as having an equal is to fall into an intellectual absurdity.

The divine attributes are what we know to be true of God. He does not possess them as qualities; they are how God is as He reveals Himself to His creatures. Love, for instance, is not something God has and which may grow or diminish or cease to be. His love is the way God is, and when He loves He is simply being Himself. And so with the other attributes.

> One God! one Majesty!
> There is no God but Thee!
> Unbounded, unextended Unity!
>
> Unfathomable Sea!
> All life is out of Thee,
> And Thy life is Thy blissful Unity.
>
> *Frederick W. Faber*

Notes

1 Julian of Norwich, *Revelations of Divine Love.* (Methune & Co, Ltd, London, seventh edition, 1920) pp.14–15.
2 Matt. 5:8.
3 Thomas Traherne, *Centuries of Meditations* (P. J. and A. E. Dobell, London, 1948) p.6.
4 The Athanasian Creed.
5 1 Cor. 2:11.

4

The Holy Trinity

God of our fathers, enthroned in light, how rich, how musical is the tongue of England! Yet when we attempt to speak forth Thy wonders, our words how poor they seem and our speech how unmelodious. When we consider the fearful mystery of Thy Triune Godhead we lay our hand upon our mouth. Before that burning bush we ask not to understand, but only that we may fitly adore Thee, One God in Persons Three. Amen.

To meditate on the three Persons of the Godhead is to walk in thought through the garden eastward in Eden and to tread on holy ground. Our sincerest effort to grasp the incomprehensible mystery of the Trinity must remain for ever futile, and only by deepest reverence can it be saved from actual presumption.

Some persons who reject all they cannot explain have denied that God is a Trinity. Subjecting the Most High to their cold, level-eyed scrutiny, they conclude that it is impossible that He could be both One and Three. These forget that their whole life is enshrouded in mystery. They fail to consider that any real explanation of even the simplest phenomenon in nature lies hidden in obscurity and can no more be explained than can the mystery of the Godhead.

Every man lives by faith, the non-believer as well as the saint; the one by faith in natural laws and the other by faith in God. Every man throughout his entire life constantly accepts without understanding. The most learned sage can be reduced to silence with one simple question, '*What?*' The answer to that question lies for ever in the abyss of unknowing beyond any man's ability to discover. 'God understandeth the way thereof, and he knoweth the place thereof,'[1] but mortal man never.

Thomas Carlyle, following Plato, pictures a man, a deep pagan thinker, who had grown to maturity in some hidden cave and is brought out suddenly to see the sun rise. 'What would his wonder be,' exclaims Carlyle, 'his rapt astonishment at the sight we daily witness with indifference! With the free, open sense of a child, yet with the ripe faculty of a man, his whole heart would be kindled by that sight...This green flowery rock-built earth, the trees, the mountains, rivers, many-sounding seas; that great deep sea of azure that swims overhead; the winds sweeping through it; the black cloud fashioning itself together, now pouring out fire, now hail and rain; what *is* it? Ay, what? At bottom we do not yet know; we can never know at all.'[2]

How different are we who have grown used to it, who have become jaded with a satiety of wonder. 'It is not by our superior insight that we escape the difficulty,' says Carlyle, 'it is by our superior levity, our inattention, our *want* of insight. It is by *not* thinking that we cease to wonder at it.... We call that fire of the black thundercloud 'electricity', and lecture learnedly about it, and grind the like of it out of glass and silk: but what *is* it? Whence comes it? Whither goes it? Science has done much for us; but it is a poor science that would hide from us the great deep sacred infinitude of Nescience, wither we can never penetrate, on which all science swims as a mere superficial film. This world, after all our science and sciences, is still a miracle; wonderful, inscrutable, magical and more, to whosoever will *think* of it.'

These penetrating, almost prophetic, words were written more than a century ago, but not all the breath-taking advances of science and technology since that time have invalidated one word or rendered obsolete as much as one period or comma. Still we do not know. We save face by repeating frivolously the popular jargon of science. We harness the mighty energy that rushes through our world; we subject it to fingertip control in our cars and our kitchens; we make it work for us like Aladdin's jinn, but still we do not know what it is. Secularism, materialism, and the intrusive presence of *things* have put out the light in our souls and turned us into a generation of zombies. We cover our deep ignorance with words, but we are ashamed to wonder, we are afraid to whisper 'mystery'.

The Church has not hesitated to teach the doctrine of the Trinity. Without pretending to understand, she has given her witness, she has repeated what the Holy Scriptures teach. Some deny that the Scriptures teach the Trinity of the Godhead on the ground that the whole idea of trinity in unity is a contradiction in terms; but since we cannot understand the fall of a leaf by the roadside or the hatching of a robin's egg in the nest yonder, why should the Trinity be a problem to us? 'We think more loftily of God,' says Michael de Molinos, 'by knowing that He is incomprehensible, and above our understanding, than by conceiving Him under any image, and creature beauty, according to our rude understanding.'[3]

Not all who called themselves Christians through the centuries were Trinitarians, but as the presence of God in the fiery pillar glowed above the camp of Israel throughout the wilderness journey, saying to all the world, 'These are My people,' so belief in the Trinity has since the days of the apostles shone above the Church of the First-born as she journeyed down the years. Purity and power have followed this faith. Under this banner have gone forth apostles, fathers, martyrs, mystics, hymnists, reformers, revivalists, and the seal of divine approval has rested on their lives and their labours. However they may have differed on minor matters, the doctrine of the Trinity bound them together.

What God declares the believing heart confesses without the need of further proof. Indeed, to seek proof is to admit doubt, and to obtain proof is to render faith superfluous. Everyone who possesses the gift of faith will recognise the wisdom of those daring words of one of the early Church fathers: 'I believe that Christ died for me because it is incredible; I believe that He rose from the dead because it is impossible.'

That was the attitude of Abraham, who against all evidence waxed strong in faith, giving glory to God. It was the attitude of Anselm, 'the second Augustine', one of the greatest thinkers of the Christian era, who held that faith must precede all effort to understand. Reflection upon revealed truth naturally follows the advent of faith, but faith comes first to the hearing ear, not to the cogitating mind. The believing man does not ponder the Word and arrive at faith by a process of reasoning, nor does he seek confirmation of faith from philosophy or science. His cry is,

> O earth, earth, earth, hear the word of the Lord....[4] Yea, let God be true, but every man a liar.[5]

Is this to dismiss scholarship as valueless in the sphere of revealed religion? By no means. The scholar has a vitally important task to perform within a carefully prescribed precinct. His task is to guarantee the purity of the text, to get as close as possible to the Word as originally given. He may compare scripture with scripture until he has discovered the true meaning of the text. But right there his authority ends. *He must never sit in judgement upon what is written*. He dare not bring the *meaning* of the Word before the bar of his reason. He dare not commend or condemn the Word as reasonable or unreasonable, scientific or unscientific. After the meaning is discovered, that meaning judges him; never does he judge it.

The doctrine of the Trinity is truth for the heart. The spirit of man alone can enter through the veil and penetrate into that Holy of Holies. 'Let me seek Thee in longing,' pleaded Anselm, 'let me long for Thee in seeking; let me find Thee in love, and love Thee in finding.'[6] Love and faith are at home in the mystery of the Godhead. Let reason kneel in reverence outside.

Christ did not hesitate to use the plural form when speaking of Himself along with the Father and the Spirit. 'We will come unto him, and make our abode with him.'[7] Yet again He said, 'I and my Father are one.'[8] It is most important that we think of God as Trinity in Unity, neither confounding the Persons nor dividing the Substance. Only so may we think rightly of God and in a manner worthy of Him and of our own souls.

It was our Lord's claim to equality with the Father that outraged the religionists of His day and led at last to His crucifixion. The attack on the doctrine of the Trinity two centuries later by Arius and others was also aimed at Christ's claim to deity. During the Arian controversy 318 Church fathers (many of them maimed and scarred by the physical violence suffered in earlier persecutions) met at Nicaea and adopted a statement of faith, one section of which runs:

> I believe in one Lord Jesus Christ,
> The Only-begotten Son of God,
> Begotten of Him before all ages,
> God of God, Light of Light,
> Very God of Very God,
> Begotten, not made.

> Being of one substance with the Father,
> By whom all things were made.

For more than sixteen hundred years this has stood as the final test of orthodoxy, as well it should, for it condenses in theological language the teaching of the New Testament concerning the position of the Son in the Godhead.

The Nicene Creed also pays tribute to the Holy Spirit as being Himself God and equal to the Father and the Son:

> I believe in the Holy Spirit
> The Lord and giver of life,
> Which proceedeth from the Father and the Son,
> Who with the Father and Son together
> Is worshipped and glorified.

Apart from the question of whether the Spirit proceeds from the Father alone or from the Father and Son, this tenet of the ancient creed has been held by the Eastern and Western branches of the Church and by all but a tiny minority of Christians.

The authors of the Athanasian Creed spelled out with great care the relation of the three Persons to each other, filling in the gaps in human thought as far as they were able while staying within the bounds of the inspired Word. 'In this Trinity,' runs the Creed, 'nothing is before or after, nothing is greater or less: but all three Persons coeternal, together and equal.'

How do these words harmonise with the saying of Jesus, 'My Father is greater than I?'[9] Those old theologians knew, and wrote into the Creed, 'Equal to His Father, as touching His Godhead; less than the Father, as touching His manhood,' and this interpretation commends itself to every serious-minded seeker after truth in a region where the light is all but blinding.

To redeem mankind the Eternal Son did not leave the bosom of the Father; while walking among men He referred to Himself as 'the only begotten Son, which is in the bosom of the Father',[10] and spoke of Himself again as 'the Son of man which is in heaven'.[11] We grant mystery here, but not confusion. In His incarnation the Son veiled His deity, but He did not void it. The unity of the Godhead made it impossible that He should surrender anything of His deity. When He took upon Him the nature of man, He did not degrade Himself or become even for a time less than He had been before. God can never become less than Himself. For God to become anything that He has not been is unthinkable.

The Persons of the Godhead, being one, have one will. They work always together, and never one smallest act is done by one without the instant acquiescence of the other two. Every act of God is accomplished by the Trinity in Unity. Here, of course, we are being driven by necessity to conceive of God in human terms. We are thinking of God by analogy with man, and the result must fall short of ultimate truth; yet if we are to think of God at all, we must do it by adapting creature-thoughts and creature-words to the Creator. It is a real if understandable error to conceive of the Persons of the Godhead as conferring with one another and reaching agreement by interchange of thought as humans do. It has always seemed to me that Milton introduces an element of weakness into his celebrated *Paradise Lost* when he presents the Persons of the Godhead conversing with each other about the redemption of the human race.

When the Son of God walked the earth as the Son of Man, He spoke often to the Father and the Father answered Him again; as the Son of Man, He now intercedes with God for His people. The dialogue involving the Father and the Son recorded in the Scriptures is always to be understood as being between the eternal Father and the man Christ Jesus. That instant, immediate communion between the Persons of the Godhead which has been from all eternity knows not sound nor effort nor motion.

> Amid the eternal silences
> God's endless Word was spoken;
> None heard but He who always spake,
> And the silence was unbroken.
>
> O marvellous! O worshipful!
> No song or sound is heard,
> But everywhere and every hour
> In love, in wisdom, and in power,
> The Father speaks His dear Eternal Word.
>
> *Frederick W. Faber*

A popular belief among Christians divides the work of God between the three Persons, giving a specific part to each, as, for instance, creation to the Father, redemption to the Son, and regeneration to the Holy Spirit. This is partly true but not wholly so, for God cannot so divide Himself that one Person works while another is inactive. In the Scriptures the three Persons are shown to act in harmonious unity in all the mighty works that are wrought throughout the universe.

In the Holy Scriptures the work of *creation* is attributed to the Father (Gen 1:1), to the Son (Col 1:16), and to the Holy Spirit (Job 26:13 and Ps 104:30). The *incarnation* is shown to have been accomplished by the three Persons in full accord (Lk 1:35), though only the Son became flesh to dwell among us. At Christ's *baptism* the Son came up out of the water, the Spirit descended upon Him and the Father's voice spoke from heaven (Matt 3:16, 17). Probably the most beautiful description of the work of *atonement* is found in Hebrews 9:14, where it is stated that Christ, through the Eternal Spirit, offered Himself without spot to God; and there we behold the three Persons operating together.

The *resurrection* of Christ is likewise attributed variously to the Father (Acts 2:32), to the Son (Jn 10:17, 18), and to the Holy Spirit (Rom 1:4). The *salvation* of the individual man is shown by the apostle Peter to be the work of all three Persons of the Godhead (1 Pet 1:2), and the *indwelling* of the Christian man's soul is said to be by the Father, the Son, and the Holy Spirit (Jn 14:15–23).

The doctrine of the Trinity, as I have said before, is truth for the heart. The fact that it cannot be satisfactorily explained, instead of being against it, is in its favour. Such a truth had to be revealed; no one could have imagined it.

O Blessed Trinity!
O simplest Majesty! O Three in One!
Thou art for ever God alone.
Holy Trinity!
Blessed equal Three.
One God, we praise Thee.
Frederick W. Faber

Notes

1 Job 28:23.
2 Thomas Carlyle, *Heroes and Hero Worship* (Henry Altemus Co, Philadelphia) pp.14–15.
3 Michael de Molinos, *op. cit.* p.58.
4 Jer. 22:29.
5 Rom. 3:4.
6 St Anselm, *Proslogium.* (Open Court Publishing Co, LaSalle, Ill, 1903) p.6.
7 John 14:23.
8 John 10:30.
9 John 14:28.
10 John 1:18.
11 John 3:13.

5

The Self-existence of God

Lord of all being! Thou alone canst affirm I AM THAT I AM: yet we who are made in Thine image may each one repeat 'I am', so confessing that we derive from Thee and that our words are but an echo of Thine own. We acknowledge Thee to be the great Original of which we through Thy goodness are grateful if imperfect copies. We worship Thee, O Father Everlasting. Amen.

'God has no origin,' said Novatian,[1] and it is precisely this concept of no-origin which distinguishes that-which-is God from whatever is not God.

Origin is a word that can apply only to things created. When we think of anything that has origin we are not thinking of God. God is self-existent, while all created things necessarily originated somewhere at some time. Aside from God, nothing is self-caused.

By our effort to discover the origin of things we confess our belief that everything was made by Someone who was made of none. By familiar experience we are taught that everything 'came from' something else. Whatever exists must have had a cause that antedates it and was at least equal to it, since the lesser cannot produce the greater. Any person or thing may be at once both caused and the cause of someone or something else; and so, back to the One who is the cause of all but is Himself caused by none.

The child by his question, 'Where did God come from?' is unwittingly acknowledging his creaturehood. Already the concept of cause and source and origin is firmly fixed in his mind. He knows that everything around him came from something other than itself, and he simply extends that concept upward to God. The little philosopher is thinking in true creature-idiom and, allowing for his lack of basic information, he is reasoning correctly. He must be told that God has no origin, and he will find this hard to grasp since it introduces a category with which he is wholly unfamiliar and contradicts the bent toward origin-seeking so deeply ingrained in all intelligent beings, a bent that impels them to probe ever back and back toward undiscovered beginnings.

To think steadily of that to which the idea of origin cannot apply is not easy, if indeed it is possible at all. Just as under certain conditions a tiny point of light can be seen, not by looking directly at it but by focusing the eyes slightly to one side, so it is with the idea of the Uncreated. When we try to focus our thought upon One who is pure uncreated being we may see nothing at all, for He dwelleth in light that no man can approach unto. Only by faith and love are we able to glimpse Him as He passes by our shelter in the cleft of the rock. 'And although this knowledge is very cloudy, vague and general,' says Michael de Molinos, 'yet, being supernatural, it produces a far more clear and perfect cognition of God than any sensible or particular apprehension that can be formed in this life; since all corporeal and sensible images are immeasurably remote from God.'[2]

The human mind, being created, has an understandable uneasiness about the Uncreated. We do not find it comfortable to allow for the presence of One who is wholly outside of the circle of our familiar knowledge. We tend to be disquieted by the thought of One who does not account to us for His being, who is responsible to no one, who is self-existent, self-dependent and self-sufficient.

Philosophy and science have not always been friendly toward the idea of God, the reason being that they are dedicated to the task of accounting for things and are impatient with anything that refuses to give an account of itself. The philosopher and the scientist will admit that there is much that they do not know; but that is quite another thing from admitting that there is something which they can *never* know, which indeed they have no technique for discovering. To admit that there is One who lies beyond us, who exists outside of all our categories, who will not be dismissed with a name, who will not appear before the bar of our reason, nor submit to our curious inquiries: this requires a great deal of humility, more than most of us possess, so we save face by thinking God down to our level, or at least down to where we can manage Him. Yet how He eludes us! For He is everywhere while He is nowhere, for 'where' has to do with matter and space, and God is independent of both. He is unaffected by time or motion, is wholly self-dependent and owes nothing to the worlds His hands have made.

Timeless, spaceless, single, lonely,
  Yet sublimely Three,
Thou art grandly, always, only
  God in Unity!
Lone in grandeur, lone in glory,
Who shall tell Thy wondrous story?
  Awful Trinity!

Frederick W. Faber

It is not a cheerful thought that millions of us, who live in a land of Bibles, who belong to churches and labour to promote the Christian religion, may yet pass our whole life on this earth without once having thought or tried to think seriously about the being of God. Few of us have let our hearts gaze in wonder at the I AM, the self-existent

Self behind which no creature can think. Such thoughts are too painful for us. We prefer to think where it will do more good – about how to build a better mousetrap, for instance, or how to make two blades of grass grow where one grew before. And for this we are now paying a too heavy price in the secularisation of our religion and the decay of our inner lives.

Perhaps some sincere but puzzled Christian may at this juncture wish to inquire about the practicality of such concepts as I am trying to set forth here. 'What bearing does this have on *my* life?' he may ask. 'What possible meaning can the self-existence of God have for me and others like me in a world such as this and in times such as these?'

To this I reply that, because we are the handiwork of God, it follows that *all our problems and their solutions are theological*. Some knowledge of what kind of God it is that operates the universe is indispensable to a sound philosophy of life and a sane outlook on the world scene. The much-quoted advice of Alexander Pope,

> Know then thyself, presume not God to scan:
> The proper study of mankind is man,

if followed literally would destroy any possibility of man's ever knowing himself in any but the most superficial way. We can never know who or what we are till we know at least something of what God is. For this reason the self-existence of God is not a wisp of dry doctrine, academic and remote; it is in fact as near as our breath and as practical as the latest surgical technique.

For reasons known only to Himself, God honoured man above all other beings by creating him in His own image. And let it be understood that the divine image in man is not a poetic fancy, not an idea born of religious longing. It is a solid theological fact, taught plainly throughout the sacred Scriptures and recognised by the Church as a truth necessary to a right understanding of the Christian faith.

Man is a created being, a derived and contingent self, who of himself possess nothing but is dependent each moment for his existence upon the One who created him after His own likeness. The fact of God is necessary to the fact of man. Think God away and man has no ground of existence.

That God is everything and man nothing is a basic tenet of Christian faith and devotion; and here the teachings of Christianity coincide with those of the more advanced and philosophical religions of the East. Man for all his genius is but an echo of the original voice, a reflection of the uncreated light. As a sunbeam perishes when cut off from the sun, so man apart from God would pass back into the void of nothingness from which he first leaped at the creative call.

Not man only, but everything that exists came out of and is dependent upon the continuing creative impulse.

> In the beginning was the Word, and the Word was with God, and the Word was God.... All things were made by him and without him was not any thing made that was made.[3]

That is how John explains it, and with him agrees the apostle Paul:

> For by him were all things created, that are in heaven and that are in earth, visible and invisible, whether they be thrones, or dominions, or principalities, or powers: all things were created by him, and for him; and he is before all things, and by him all things consist.[4]

To this witness the writer to the Hebrews adds his voice, testifying of Christ that He is the brightness of God's glory and the express image of His Person, and that He upholds all things by the word of His power.

In his utter dependence of all things upon the creative will of God lies the possibility for both holiness and sin. One of the marks of God's image in man is his ability to exercise moral choice. The teaching of Christianity is that man chose to be independent of God and confirmed his choice by deliberately disobeying a divine command. This act violated the relationship that normally existed between God and His creature; it rejected God as the ground of existence and threw man back upon himself. Thereafter he became not a planet revolving around the central Sun, but a sun in his own right, around which everything else must revolve.

A more positive assertion of selfhood could not be imagined than those words of God to Moses:

> I AM THAT I AM.[5]

Everything God is, everything that is God, is set forth in that unqualified declaration of independent being. Yet in God, self is not sin but the quintessence of all possible goodness, holiness and truth.

The natural man is a sinner because and only because he challenges God's selfhood in relation to his own. In all else he may willingly accept the sovereignty of God; in his own life he rejects it. For him, God's dominion ends where his begins. For him, self becomes Self, and in this he unconsciously imitates Lucifer, that fallen son of the morning who said in his heart,

> I will ascend into heaven, I will exalt my throne above the stars of God. . . . I will be like the most High.[6]

Yet so subtle is self that scarcely anyone is conscious of its presence. Because man is born a rebel, he is unaware that he is one. His constant assertion of self, as far as he thinks of it at all, appears to him a perfectly normal thing. He is willing to share himself, sometimes even to sacrifice himself for a desired end, but never to dethrone himself. No matter how far down the scale of social acceptance he may slide, he is still in his own eyes a king on a throne, and no one, not even God, can take that throne from him.

Sin has many manifestations but its essence is one. A moral being, created to worship before the throne of God, sits on the throne of his own selfhood and from that elevated position declares 'I AM.' That is sin in its concentrated essence; yet because it is natural it appears to be good. It is only when in the gospel the soul is brought before the face of the Most Holy One without the protective shield of ignorance that the frightful moral incongruity is brought home to the conscience. In the language of evangelism the man who is thus confronted by the fiery presence of Almighty God is said to be under conviction. Christ referred to this when He said of the Spirit whom He would send to the world,

> And when he is come, he will reprove the world of sin, and of righteousness, and of judgment.[7]

The earliest fulfilment of these words of Christ was at Pentecost after Peter had preached the first great Christian sermon. 'Now when they heard this, they were pricked in their heart, and said unto Peter and to the rest of the apostles, Men and brethren, what shall we do?' This 'What shall we do?'[8] is the deep heart cry of every man who suddenly realises that he is a usurper and sits on a stolen throne. However painful, it is precisely this acute moral consternation that produces true repentance and makes a robust Christian after the penitent has been dethroned and has found forgiveness and peace through the gospel.

'Purity of heart is to will one thing,' said Kierkegaard, and we may with equal truth turn this about and declare, 'The essence of sin is to will one thing,' for to set our will against the will of God is to dethrone God and make ourselves supreme in the little kingdom of Mansoul. This is sin at its evil root. Sins may multiply like the sands on the sea-shore, but they are yet one. Sins are because sin is. This is the rationale behind the much maligned doctrine of natural depravity which holds that the impenitent man can do nothing but sin and that his good deeds are really not good at all. His best religious works God rejects as He rejected the offering of Cain. Only when he has restored his stolen throne to God are his works acceptable.

The struggle of the Christian man to be good while the bent toward self-assertion still lives within him as a kind of unconscious moral reflex is vividly described by the apostle Paul in the seventh chapter of his Roman Epistle; and his testimony is in full accord with the teaching of the prophets. Eight hundred years before the advent of Christ the prophet Isaiah identified sin as rebellion against the will of God and the assertion of the right of each man to choose for himself the way he shall go. 'All we like sheep have gone astray,' he said, 'we have turned every one to his own way,'[9] and I believe that no more accurate description of sin has ever been given.

The witness of the saints has been in full harmony with prophet and apostle, that an inward principle of self lies at the source of human conduct, turning everything men do into evil. To save us completely Christ must reverse the bent of our nature; He must plant a new principle within us so that our subsequent conduct will spring out of a desire to promote the honour of God and the good of our fellow men. The old self-sins must die, and the only instrument by which they can be slain is the cross.

> If any man will come after me, let him deny himself and take up his cross, and follow me,[10]

said our Lord, and years later the victorious Paul could say,

> I am crucified with Christ: nevertheless I live; yet not I, but Christ liveth in me.[11]

> My God, shall sin its power maintain
> And in my soul defiant live!
> 'Tis not enough that Thou forgive,
> The cross must rise and self be slain.
>
> O God of love, Thy power disclose:
> 'Tis not enough that Christ should rise,
> I, too, must seek the brightening skies,
> And rise from death, as Christ arose.
>
> *Greek Hymn*

Notes

1 Novatian, *On the Trinity* (Macmillan Co, New York, 1919) p.25.
2 Michael de Molinos, *op. cit.* p.58.
3 John 1:1–3.
4 Col. 1:16–17.
5 Ex. 3:14.
6 Isa. 14:13–14.
7 John 16:8.
8 Acts 2:37.
9 Isa. 53:6.
10 Matt. 16:24.
11 Gal. 2:20.

6

The Self-sufficiency of God

Teach us, O God, that nothing is necessary to Thee. Were anything necessary to Thee that thing would be the measure of Thine imperfection: and how could we worship one who is imperfect? If nothing is necessary to Thee, then no one is necessary, and if no one, then not we. Thou dost seek us though Thou dost not need us. We seek Thee because we need Thee, for in Thee we live and move and have our being. Amen.

'The Father hath life in himself,'[1] said our Lord, and it is characteristic of His teaching that He thus in a brief sentence sets forth truth so lofty as to transcend the highest reaches of human thought. God, He said, is self-sufficient; He is what He is *in Himself*, in the final meaning of those words.

Whatever God is, and all that God is, He is in Himself. All life is in and from God, whether it be the lowest form of unconscious life or the highly self-conscious, intelligent life of a seraph. No creature has life in itself; all life is a gift from God.

The life of God, conversely, is not a gift from another. Were there another from whom God could receive the gift of life, or indeed any gift whatever, that other would be God in fact. An elementary but correct way to think of God is as the One who contains all, who gives all that is given, but who Himself can receive nothing that He has not first given.

To admit the existence of a need in God is to admit incompleteness in the divine being. Need is a creature-word and cannot be spoken of the Creator. God has a voluntary relation to everything He has made, but He has no *necessary* relation to anything outside of Himself. His interest in His creatures arises from His sovereign good pleasure, not from any need those creatures can supply nor from any completeness they can bring to Him who is complete in Himself.

Again we must reverse the familiar flow of our thoughts and try to understand that which is unique, that which stands alone as being true in this situation and nowhere else. Our common habits of thought allow for the existence of need among created things. Nothing is complete in itself but requires something outside itself in order to exist. All breathing things need air; every organism needs food and water. Take air and water from the earth and all life would perish instantly. It may be stated as an axiom that to stay alive every created thing needs some other created thing and all things need God. To God alone nothing is necessary.

The river grows larger by its tributaries, but where is the tributary that can enlarge the One out of whom came everything and to whose infinite fullness all creation owes its being?

> Unfathomable Sea: all life is out of Thee,
> And Thy life is Thy blissful Unity.
>
> *Frederick W. Faber*

The problem of why God created the universe still troubles thinking men; but if we cannot know why, we can at least know that He did not bring His worlds into being to meet some unfulfilled need in Himself, as a man might build a house to shelter him against the winter cold or plant a field of corn to provide him with necessary food. The word *necessary* is wholly foreign to God.

Since He is the being supreme over all, it follows that God cannot be elevated. Nothing is above Him, nothing beyond Him. Any motion in His direction is elevation for the creature; away from Him, descent. He holds His position out of Himself and by leave of none. As no one can promote Him, so no one can degrade Him. It is written that He upholds all things by the word of His power. How can He be raised or supported by the things He upholds?

Were all human beings suddenly to become blind, still the sun would shine by day and the stars by night, for these owe nothing to the millions who benefit from their light. So, were every man on earth to become atheist, it could not affect God in any way. He is what He is in Himself without regard to any other. To believe in Him adds nothing to His perfections; to doubt Him takes nothing away.

Almighty God, just because He is almighty, needs no support. The picture of a nervous, ingratiating God fawning over men to win their favour is not a pleasant one; yet if we look at the popular conception of God that is precisely what we see. Twentieth-century Christianity has put God on charity. So lofty is our opinion of ourselves that we find it quite easy, not to say enjoyable, to believe that we are necessary to God. But the truth is that God is not greater for our being, nor would He be less if we did not exist. That we do exist is altogether of God's free determination, not by our desert nor by divine necessity.

Probably the hardest thought of all for our natural egotism to entertain is that God does not need our help. We commonly represent Him as a busy, eager, somewhat frustrated Father hurrying about seeking help to carry out

His benevolent plan to bring peace and salvation to the world; but, as said the Lady Julian, 'I saw truly that God doeth all-thing, be it never so little.'[2]

The God who worketh all things surely needs no help and no helpers.

Too many missionary appeals are based upon this fancied frustration of Almighty God. An effective speaker can easily excite pity in his hearers, not only for the heathen but for the God who has tried so hard and so long to save them and has failed for want of support. I fear that thousands of young persons enter Christian service from no higher motive than to help deliver God from the embarrassing situation His love has got Him into and His limited abilities seem unable to get Him out of. Add to this a certain degree of commendable idealism and a fair amount of compassion for the underprivileged and you have the true drive behind much Christian activity today.

Again, God needs no defenders. He is the eternal undefended. To communicate with us in an idiom we can understand, God in the Scriptures makes full use of military terms; but surely it was never intended that we should think of the throne of the Majesty on high as being under siege, with Michael and his hosts or some other heavenly beings defending it from stormy overthrow. So to think is to misunderstand everything the Bible would tell us about God. Neither Judaism nor Christianity could approve such puerile notions. A God who must be defended is one who can help us only while someone is helping Him. We may count upon Him only if He wins in the cosmic see-saw battle between right and wrong. Such a God could not command the respect of intelligent men; He could only excite their pity.

To be right we must think worthily of God. It is morally imperative that we purge from our minds all ignoble concepts of the Diety and let Him be the God in our minds that He is in His universe. The Christian religion has to do with God and man, but its focal point is God, not man. Man's only claim to importance is that he was created in the divine image; in himself he is nothing. The psalmists and prophets of the Scriptures refer in sad scorn to weak man whose breath is in his nostrils, who grows up like the grass in the morning only to be cut down and wither before the setting of the sun. That God exists for Himself and man for the glory of God is the emphatic teaching of the Bible. The high honour of God is first in heaven as it must yet be in earth.

From all this we may begin to understand why the Holy Scriptures have so much to say about the vital place of faith and why they brand unbelief as a deadly sin. Among all created beings, not one dare trust in itself. God alone trusts in Himself; all other beings must trust in Him. Unbelief is actually perverted faith, for it puts its trust not in the living God but in dying men. The unbeliever denies the self-sufficiency of God and usurps attributes that are not his. This dual sin dishonours God and ultimately destroys the soul of the man.

In His love and pity God came to us as Christ. This has been the consistent position of the Church from the days of the apostles. It is fixed for Christian belief in the doctrine of the incarnation of the Eternal Son. In recent times, however, this has come to mean something different from, and less than, what it meant to the early church. The man Jesus as He appeared in the flesh has been equated with the Godhead and all His human weaknesses and limitations attributed to the Deity. The truth is that the man who walked among us was a demonstration, not of unveiled deity but of perfect humanity. The awful majesty of the Godhead was mercifully sheathed in the soft envelope of human nature to protect mankind. 'Go down,' God told Moses on the mountain, 'charge the people, lest they break through unto the Lord to gaze, and many of them perish';[3] and later, 'Thou canst not see my face: for there shall no man see me, and live.'[4]

Christians today appear to know Christ only after the flesh. They try to achieve communion with Him by divesting Him of His burning holiness and unapproachable majesty, the very attributes He veiled while on earth but assumed in fullness of glory upon His ascension to the Father's right hand. The Christ of popular Christianity has a weak smile and a halo. He has become Someone-up-There who likes people, at least some people, and these are grateful but not too impressed. If they need Him, He also needs them.

Let us not imagine that the truth of the divine self-sufficiency will paralyse Christian activity. Rather it will stimulate all holy endeavour. This truth, while a needed rebuke to human self-confidence, will when viewed in its biblical perspective lift from our minds the exhausting load of mortality and encourage us to take the easy yoke of Christ and spend ourselves in Spirit-inspired toil for the honour of God and the good of mankind. For the blessed news is that the God who needs no one has in sovereign condescension stooped to work by and in and through His obedient children.

If all this appears self-contradictory – *Amen*, be it so. The various elements of truth stand in perpetual antithesis, sometimes requiring us to believe apparent opposites while we wait for the moment when we shall know as we are known. Then truth which now appears to be in conflict with itself will arise in shining unity and it will be seen that the conflict has not been in the truth but in our sin-damaged minds.

In the meanwhile our inner fulfilment lies in loving obedience to the commandments of Christ and the inspired admonitions of His apostles.

It is God which worketh in you.[5]

He needs no one, but when faith is present *He works through anyone*. Two statements are in this sentence and a healthy spiritual life requires that we accept both. For a full generation the first has been in almost total eclipse, and that to our deep spiritual injury.

> Fountain of good, all blessing flows
> From Thee; no want Thy fullness knows;
> What but Thyself canst Thou desire?
> Yet, self-sufficient as Thou art,
> Thou dost desire my worthless heart;
> This, only this, dost Thou require.
>
> *Johann Scheffler*

Notes

1 John 5:26.
2 Julian of Norwich, *op. cit.* p.27.
3 Ex. 19:21.
4 Ex. 33:20.
5 Phil. 2:13.

7

The Eternity of God

This day our hearts approve with gladness what our reason can never fully comprehend, even Thine eternity, O Ancient of Days. Art Thou not from everlasting, O Lord, my God, mine Holy One?

We worship Thee, the Father Everlasting, whose years shall have no end; and Thee, the love-begotten Son whose goings forth have been ever of old; we also acknowledge and adore Thee, Eternal Spirit, who before the foundation of the world didst live and love in coequal glory with the Father and the Son.

Enlarge and purify the mansions of our souls that they may be fit habitations for Thy Spirit, who dost prefer before all temples the upright heart and pure. Amen.

The concept of everlastingness runs like a lofty mountain range throughout the entire Bible and looms large in orthodox Hebrew and Christian thought. Were we to reject the concept, it would be altogether impossible for us to think again the thoughts of prophets and apostles, so full were they of the long dreams of eternity.

Because the word *everlasting* is sometimes used by the sacred writers to mean no more than long-lasting (as 'the everlasting hills'),[1] some persons have argued that the concept of unending existence was not in the minds of the writers when they used the word but was supplied later by the theologians. This is of course a serious error, and, as far as I can see, has no ground in serious scholarship. It has been used by certain teachers as an escape from the doctrine of eternal punishment. These reject the eternity of moral retribution, and to be consistent they are forced to weaken the whole idea of endlessness. This is not the only instance where an attempt was made to slay a truth to keep it quiet lest it appear as a material witness against an error.

The truth is that if the Bible did not teach that God possessed endless being in the ultimate meaning of that term, we would be compelled to infer it from His other attributes, and if the Holy Scriptures had no word for absolute everlastingness, it would be necessary for us to coin one to express the concept, for it is assumed, implied, and generally taken for granted everywhere throughout the inspired Scriptures. The idea of endlessness is to the kingdom of God what carbon is to the kingdom of nature. As carbon is present almost everywhere, as it is an essential element in all living matter and supplies all life with energy, so the concept of everlastingness is necessary to give meaning to any Christian doctrine. Indeed I know of no tenet of the Christian creed that could retain its significance if the idea of eternity were extracted from it.

'From everlasting to everlasting, thou art God,'[2] said Moses in the Spirit. 'From the vanishing point to the vanishing point' would be another way to say it quite in keeping with the words as Moses used them. The mind looks backward in time till the dim past vanishes, then turns and looks into the future till thought and imagination collapse from exhaustion; and God is at both points, unaffected by either. Time marks the beginning of created existence, and because God never began to exist it can have no application to Him. 'Began' is a time-word, and can have no personal meaning for the high and lofty One that inhabiteth eternity.

No age can heap its outward years on Thee;
Dear God! Thou art, Thyself, Thine own eternity.
Frederick W. Faber

Because God lives in an everlasting now, He has no past and no future. When time-words occur in the Scriptures they refer to our time, not to His. When the four living creatures before the throne cry day and night,

> Holy, holy, holy, Lord God Almighty, which was, and is, and is to come,[3]

they are identifying God with the flow of creature-life with its familiar three tenses; and this is right and good, for God has sovereignly willed so to identify Himself. But since God is uncreated, He is not Himself affected by that succession of consecutive changes we call time.

God dwells in eternity but time dwells in God. He has already lived all our tomorrows as He has lived all our yesterdays. An illustration offered by C. S. Lewis may help us here. He suggests that we think of a sheet of paper infinitely extended. That would be eternity. Then on that paper draw a short line to represent time. As the line begins and ends on that infinite expanse, so time began in God and will end in Him.

That God appears at time's beginning is not too difficult to comprehend, but that He appears at the beginning and end of time *simultaneously* is not so easy to grasp; yet it is true. Time is known to us by a succession of events. It is the way we account for consecutive changes in the universe. Changes take place not all at once but in succession, one after the other, and it is the relation of 'after' to 'before' that gives us our idea of time. We wait for the sun to move from east to west or for the hour hand to move around the face of the clock, but God is not compelled so to wait. For Him everything that will happen has already happened.

This is why God can say,

> I am God, and there is none like me, declaring the end from the beginning.[4]

He sees the end and the beginning in one view. 'For infinite duration, which is eternity's self, includeth all succession,' says Nicholas of Cusa, 'and all which seemeth to us to be in succession existeth not posterior to Thy concept, which is eternity.... Thus, because Thou art God Almighty, Thou dwellest within the wall of Paradise, and this wall is that coincidence where later is one with earlier, where the end is one with the beginning, where Alpha and Omega are the same.... For NOW and THEN coincide in the circle of the wall of Paradise. But, O my God, the absolute and eternal, it is beyond the present and the past that Thou dost exist and utter speech.'[5]

When he was a very old man, Moses wrote the psalm from which I have quoted earlier in this chapter. In it he celebrates the eternity of God. To him this truth is a solid theological fact as firm and hard as that Mount Sinai with which he was so familiar, and for him it had two practical meanings: since God is eternal, He can be and continue for ever to be the one safe home for His time-driven children.

> Lord, thou hast been our dwelling place in all generations.[6]

The second thought is less comforting: God's eternity is so long and our years on earth are so few, how shall we establish the work of our hands? How shall we escape the abrasive action of events that would wear us out and destroy us? God fills and dominates the psalm, so it is to Him that Moses makes his plaintive appeal,

> So teach us to number our days, that we may apply our hearts unto wisdom.[7]

May the knowledge of Thy eternity not be wasted on me!

We who live in this nervous age would be wise to meditate on our lives and our days long and often before the face of God and on the edge of eternity. For we are made for eternity as certainly as we are made for time, and as responsible moral beings we must deal with both.

'He hath set eternity in their heart,'[8] said the preacher, and I think he here sets forth both the glory and the misery of men. To be made for eternity and forced to dwell in time is for mankind a tragedy of huge proportions. All within us cries for life and permanence, and everything around us reminds us of mortality and change. Yet that God has made us of the stuff of eternity is both a glory and a prophecy, a glory yet to be realised and a prophecy yet to be fulfilled.

I hope it will not be found unduly repetitious if I return again to that important pillar of Christian theology, the image of God in man. The marks of the divine image have been so obscured by sin that they are not easy to identify, but is it not reasonable to believe that one mark may be man's insatiable craving for immortality?

> Thou wilt not leave us in the dust:
> Thou madest man, he knows not why;
> He thinks he was not made to die
> And Thou hast made him: Thou art just.[9]

So reasons Tennyson, and the deepest instincts of the normal human heart agree with him. The ancient image of God whispers within every man of everlasting hope; somewhere he will continue to exist. Still he cannot rejoice, for the light that lighteth every man that cometh into the world troubles his conscience, frightening him with proofs of guilt and evidences of coming death. So is he ground between the upper millstone of hope and the nether stone of fear.

Just here the sweet relevancy of the Christian message appears.

> Jesus Christ...hath abolished death, and hath brought life and immortality to light through the gospel.[10]

So wrote the greatest Christian of them all just before he went out to meet his executioner. God's eternity and man's mortality join to persuade us that faith in Jesus Christ is not optional. For every man it must be Christ or eternal tragedy. Out of eternity our Lord came into time to rescue His human brethren whose moral folly had made them not only fools of the passing world but slaves of sin and death as well.

Brief life is here our portion,
  Brief sorrow, short-lived care;
The life that knows no ending,
  The tearless life is there.

There God, our King and Portion,
  In fullness of His grace,
We then shall see for ever,
  And worship face to face.

Bernard of Cluny

Notes

1 Gen. 49:26.
2 Ps. 90:2.
3 Rev. 4:8.
4 Isa. 46:9–10.
5 Nicholas of Cusa, *op. cit.* pp.48, 49, 50.
6 Ps. 90:1.
7 Ps. 90:12.
8 Eccles. 3:11 ASV.
9 Tennyson, *In Memoriam*.
10 2 Tim. 1:10.

8

God's Infinitude

Our Heavenly Father: Let us see Thy glory, if it must be from the shelter of the cleft rock and from beneath the protection of Thy covering hand. Whatever the cost to us in loss of friends or goods or length of days let us know Thee as Thou art, that we may adore Thee as we should. Through Jesus Christ our Lord. Amen.

The world is evil, the times are waxing late, and the glory of God has departed from the church as the fiery cloud once lifted from the door of the temple in the sight of Ezekiel the prophet.

The God of Abraham has withdrawn His conscious presence from us, and another god whom our fathers knew not is making himself at home among us. This god we have made and because we have made him we can understand him; because we have created him he can never surprise us, never overwhelm us, nor astonish us, nor transcend us.

The God of glory sometimes revealed Himself like a sun to warm and bless, indeed, but often to astonish, overwhelm, and blind before He healed and bestowed permanent sight. This God of our fathers wills to be the God of their succeeding race. We have only to prepare Him a habitation in love and faith and humility. We have but to want Him badly enough, and He will come and manifest Himself to us.

Shall we allow a saintly and thoughtful man to exhort us? Hear Anselm; or better still, heed his words:

> Up now, slight man! Flee for a little while thy occupations; hide thyself for a time from thy disturbing thoughts. Cast aside now thy burdensome cares, and put away thy toilsome business. Yield room for some little time to God, and rest for a little time in Him. Enter the inner chamber of thy mind; shut out all thoughts save that of God and such as can aid thee in seeking Him. Speak now, my whole heart! Speak now to God, saying, I seek Thy face; Thy face, Lord, will I seek.[1]

Of all that can be thought or said about God, His infinitude is the most difficult to grasp. Even to try to conceive of it would appear to be self-contradictory, for such conceptualisation requires us to undertake something which we know at the outset we can never accomplish. Yet we must try, for the Holy Scriptures teach that God is infinite and, if we accept His other attributes, we must of necessity accept this one too.

From the effort to understand, we must not turn back because the way is difficult and there are no mechanical aids for the ascent. The view is better farther up and the journey is not one for the feet but for the heart. Let us seek, therefore, such 'trances of thought and mountings of the mind' as God may be pleased to grant us, knowing that the Lord often pours eyesight on the blind and whispers to babes and sucklings truths never dreamed of by the wise and prudent. Now the blind must see and the deaf hear. Now we must expect to receive the treasures of darkness and the hidden riches of secret places.

Infinitude, of course, means limitlessness, and it is obviously impossible for a limited mind to grasp the Unlimited. In this chapter I am compelled to think one step short of that about which I am writing, and the reader must of necessity think a degree under that about which he is trying to think. O, the depths of the riches both of the wisdom and knowledge of God! How unsearchable are His judgements, and His ways past finding out!

The reason for our dilemma has been suggested before. We are trying to envision a mode of being altogether foreign to us, and wholly unlike anything we have known in our familiar world of matter, space, and time.

'Here, and in all our meditations upon the qualities and content of God,' writes Novatian, 'we pass beyond our power of fit conception, nor can human eloquence put forth a power to commensurate with His greatness. At the contemplation and utterance of His majesty all eloquence is rightly dumb, all mental effort is feeble. For God is greater than mind itself. His greatness cannot be conceived. Nay, could we conceive of His greatness He would be less than the human mind which could form the conception. He is greater than all language, and no statement can express Him. Indeed, if any statement could express Him, He would be less than human speech which could by such statement comprehend and gather up all that He is. All our thoughts about Him will be less than He, and our loftiest utterances will be trivialities in comparison with Him.'[2]

Unfortunately the word *infinite* has not always been held to its precise meaning, but has been used carelessly to mean simply *much* or a *great deal*, as when we say that an artist takes infinite pains with his picture or a teacher shows infinite patience with her class. Properly, the word can be used of no created thing, and of no one but God. Hence, to argue about whether or not space is infinite is to play with words. Infinitude can belong to but One. There can be no second.

When we say that God is infinite we mean that He knows *no bounds*. Whatever God is and all that God is, He is without limit. And here again we must break away from the popular meaning of words. 'Unlimited wealth' and 'boundless energy' are further examples of the misuse of words. Of course no wealth is unlimited and no energy boundless unless we are speaking of the wealth and energy of God.

Again, to say that God is infinite is to say that He is *measureless*. Measurement is the way created things have of accounting for themselves. It describes limitations, imperfections, and cannot apply to God. Weight describes the gravitational pull of the earth upon material bodies; distance describes intervals between bodies in space; length means extension in space, and there are other familiar measurements such as those for liquid, energy, sound, light, and numbers for pluralities. We also try to measure abstract qualities, and speak of great or little faith, high or low intelligence, large or meagre talents.

Is it not plain that all this does not and cannot apply to God? It is the way we see the works of His hands, but not the way we see Him. He is above all this, outside of it, beyond it. Our concepts of measurement embrace mountains and men, atoms and stars, gravity, energy, numbers, speed, but never God. We cannot speak of measure or amount or size or weight and at the same time be speaking of God, for these tell of degrees and there are no degrees in God. All that He is He is without growth or addition or development. Nothing in God is less or more, or large or small. He is what He is in Himself, without qualifying thought or word. He is simply God.

In the awful abyss of the divine being may lie attributes of which we know nothing and which can have no meaning for us, just as the attributes of mercy and grace can have no personal meaning for seraphim or cherubim. These holy beings may know of these qualities in God but be unable to feel them sympathetically for the reason that they have not sinned and so do not call forth God's mercy and grace. So there may be, and I believe there surely are, other aspects of God's essential being which He has not revealed even to His ransomed and Spirit-illuminated children. These hidden facets of God's nature concern His relation to none but Himself. They are like the far side of the moon, which we know is there but which has never been explored and has no immediate meaning for men on earth. There is no reason for us to try to discover what has not been revealed. It is enough to know that God is God.

> Thine own Self for ever filling
> With self-kindled flame,
> In Thyself Thou art distilling
> Unctions without name!
> Without worshipping of creatures,
> Without veiling of Thy features,
> God always the same!
>
> *Frederick W. Faber*

But God's infinitude belongs to us and is made known to us for our everlasting profit. Yet, just *what* does it mean to us beyond the mere wonder of thinking about it? Much every way, and more as we come to know ourselves and God better.

Because God's nature is infinite, everything that flows out of it is infinite also. We poor human creatures are constantly being frustrated by limitations imposed upon us from without and within. The days of the years of our lives are few, and swifter than a weaver's shuttle. Life is a short and fevered rehearsal for a concert we cannot stay to give. Just when we appear to have attained some proficiency we are forced to lay our instruments down. There is simply not time enough to think, to become, to perform what the constitution of our natures indicates we are capable of.

How completely satisfying to turn from our limitations to a God who has none. Eternal years lie in His heart. For Him time does not pass, it remains; and those who are in

Christ share with Him all the riches of limitless time and endless years. God never hurries. There are no deadlines against which He must work. Only to know this is to quiet our spirits and relax our nerves. For those out of Christ, time is a devouring beast; before the sons of the new creation time crouches and purrs and licks their hands. The foe of the old human race becomes the friend of the new, and the stars in their courses fight for the man God delights to honour. This we may learn from the divine infinitude.

But there is more. God's gifts in nature have their limitations. They are finite because they have been created, but the gift of eternal life in Christ Jesus is as limitless as God. The Christian man possesses God's own life and shares His infinitude with Him. In God there is life enough for all and time enough to enjoy it. Whatever is possessed of natural life runs through its cycle from birth to death and ceases to be, but the life of God returns upon itself and ceases never. And this is life eternal: to know the only true God, and Jesus Christ whom He has sent.

The mercy of God is infinite too, and the man who has felt the grinding pain of inward guilt knows that this is more than academic.

> Where sin abounded, grace did much more abound.[3]

Abounding sin is the terror of the world, but abounding grace is the hope of mankind. However sin may abound it still has its limits, for it is the product of finite minds and hearts; but God's 'much more' introduces us to infinitude. Against our deep creature-sickness stands God's infinite ability to cure.

The Christian witness through the centuries has been that 'God so loved the world'[4]; it remains for us to see that love in the light of God's infinitude. His love is measureless. It is more: it is boundless. It has no bounds because it is not a thing but a facet of the essential nature of God. His love is something He *is*, and because He is infinite that love can enfold the whole created world in itself and have room for ten thousand times ten thousand worlds beside.

> This, this is the God we adore,
> Our faithful, unchangeable Friend,
> Whose love is as great as His power,
> And neither knows measure nor end.
>
> 'Tis Jesus, the first and the last,
> Whose Spirit shall guide us safe home;
> We'll praise Him for all that is past,
> And trust Him for all that's to come.
>
> *Joseph Hart*

Notes

1 St Anselm, *op. cit.* p.3.
2 Novation, *op. cit.* pp.26–27.
3 Rom. 5:20.
4 John 3:16.

9

The Immutability of God

O Christ our Lord, Thou hast been our dwelling place in all generations. As conies to their rock, so have we run to Thee for safety; as birds from their wanderings, so have we flown to Thee for peace. Chance and change are busy in our little world of nature and men, but in Thee we find no variableness nor shadow of turning. We rest in Thee without fear or doubt and face our tomorrows without anxiety. Amen.

The immutability of God is among those attributes less difficult to understand, but to grasp it we must discipline ourselves to sort out the usual thoughts with which we think of created things from the rarer ones that arise when we try to lay hold of whatever may be comprehended of God.

To say that God is immutable is to say that He never differs from Himself. The concept of a growing or developing God is not found in the Scriptures. It seems to me impossible to think of God as varying from Himself in any way. Here is why:

For a moral being to change it would be necessary that the change be in one of three directions. He must go from better to worse or from worse to better; or, granted that the moral quality remain stable, he must change within himself, as from immature to mature or from one order of being to another. It should be clear that God can move in none of these directions. His perfections for ever rule out any such possibility.

God cannot change for the better. Since He is perfectly holy, He has never been less holy than He is now and can never be holier than He is and has always been. Neither can God change for the worse. Any deterioration within the unspeakably holy nature of God is impossible. Indeed I believe it impossible even to think of such a thing, for the moment we attempt to do so, the object about which we are thinking is no longer God but something else and someone less than He. The one of whom we are thinking may be a great and awesome creature, but because he is a creature he cannot be the self-existent Creator.

As there can be no mutation in the moral character of God, so there can be none within the divine essence. The being of God is unique in the only proper meaning of that word; that is, His being is other than and different from all other beings. We have seen how God differs from His creatures in being self-existent, self-sufficient, and eternal. By virtue of these attributes God is God and not some other being. One who can suffer any slightest degree of change is neither self-existent, self-sufficient, nor eternal, and so is not God.

Only a being composed of parts may change, for change is basically a shift in the relation of the parts of a whole or the admission of some foreign element into the original composition. Since God is self-existent, He is not composed. There are in Him no parts to be altered. And since He is self-sufficient, nothing can enter His being from without.

'Whatever is composed of parts,' says Anselm, 'is not altogether one, but is in some sort plural, and diverse from itself; and either in fact or in concept is capable of dissolution. But these things are alien to Thee, than whom nothing better can be conceived of. Hence, there are no parts in Thee, Lord, nor art Thou more than one. But

Thou art so truly a unitary being, and so identical with Thyself, that in no respect art Thou unlike Thyself; rather Thou art unity itself, indivisible by any conception.'[1]

'All that God is He has always been, and all that He has been and is He will ever be.' Nothing that God has ever said about Himself will be modified; nothing the inspired prophets and apostles have said about Him will be rescinded. His immutability guarantees this.

The immutability of God appears in its most perfect beauty when viewed against the mutability of men. In God no change is possible; in men change is impossible to escape. Neither the man is fixed nor his world, but he and it are in constant flux. Each man appears for a little while to laugh and weep, to work and play, and then to go to make room for those who shall follow him in the never-ending cycle.

Certain poets have found a morbid pleasure in the law of impermanence and have sung in a minor key the song of perpetual change. Omar the tentmaker was one who sang with pathos and humour of mutation and mortality, the twin diseases that afflict mankind. 'Don't slap that clay around so roughly,' he exhorts the potter, 'that may be your grandfather's dust you make so free with.' 'When you lift the cup to drink red wine,' he reminds the reveler, 'you may be kissing the lips of some beauty dead long ago.'

This note of sweet sorrow expressed with gentle humour gives a radiant beauty to his quatrains but, however beautiful, the whole long poem is sick, sick unto death. Like the bird charmed by the serpent that would devour it, the poet is fascinated by the enemy that is destroying him and all men and every generation of men.

The sacred writers, too, face up to man's mutability, but they are healthy men and there is a wholesome strength in their words. They have found the cure for the great sickness. God, they say, changes not. The law of mutation belongs to a fallen world, but God is immutable, and in Him men of faith find at last eternal permanence. In the meanwhile change works for the children of the kingdom, not against them. The changes that occur in them are wrought by the hand of the in-living Spirit. 'But we all,' says the apostle, 'with open face beholding as in a glass the glory of the Lord, are changed into the same image from glory to glory, even as by the Spirit of the Lord.'[2]

In a world of change and decay not even the man of faith can be completely happy. Instinctively he seeks the unchanging and is bereaved at the passing of dear familiar things.

O Lord! my heart is sick,
Sick of this everlasting change;
And life runs tediously quick
Through its unresting race and varied range:
Change finds no likeness to itself in Thee,
And wakes no echo in Thy mute Eternity.
Frederick W. Faber

These words of Faber find sympathetic response in every heart; yet much as we may deplore the lack of stability in all earthly things, in a fallen world such as this the very *ability* to change is a golden treasure, a gift from God of such fabulous worth as to call for constant thanksgiving. For human beings the whole possibility of redemption lies in their ability to change. To move across from one sort of person to another is the essence of repentance: the liar becomes truthful, the thief honest, the lewd pure, the proud humble. The whole moral texture of the life is altered. The thoughts, the desires, the affections are transformed, and the man is no longer what he had been before. So radical is this change that the apostle calls the man that used to be 'the old man' and the man that now is 'the new man, which is renewed in knowledge after the image of him that created him'.[3]

Yet the change is deeper and more basic than any external acts can reveal, for it includes also the reception of life of another and higher quality. The old man, even at his best, possesses only the life of Adam: the new man has the life of God. And this is more than a mere manner of speaking; it is quite literally true. When God infuses eternal life into the spirit of a man, the man becomes a member of a new and higher order of being.

In the working out of His redemptive process the unchanging God makes full use of change and through a succession of changes arrives at permanence at last. In the Book of Hebrews this is shown most clearly. 'He taketh away the first, that he may establish the second',[4] is a kind of summation of the teaching of that remarkable book. The old covenant, as something provisional, was abolished, and the new and everlasting covenant took its place. The blood of goats and bulls lost its significance when the blood of the Paschal Lamb was shed. The law, the altar, the priesthood – all were temporary and subject to change; now the eternal law of God is engraven for ever on the living, sensitive stuff of which the human soul is composed. The ancient sanctuary is no more, but the new sanctuary is eternal in the heavens and there the Son of God has His eternal priesthood.

Here we see that God uses change as a lowly servant to bless His redeemed household, but He Himself is outside of the law of mutation and is unaffected by any changes that occur in the universe.

> And all things as they change proclaim
> The Lord eternally the same.
>
> *Charles Wesley*

Again the question of use arises. 'Of what use to me is the knowledge that God is immutable?' someone asks. 'Is not the whole thing mere metaphysical speculation? Something that might bring a certain satisfaction to persons of a particular type of mind but can have no real significance for practical men?'

If by 'practical men' we mean unbelieving men engrossed in secular affairs and indifferent to the claims of Christ, the welfare of their own souls, or the interests of the world to come, then for them such a book as this can have no meaning at all; nor, unfortunately, can any other book that takes religion seriously. But while such men may be in the majority, they do not by any means compose the whole of the population. There are still the seven thousand who have not bowed their knees to Baal. These believe they were created to worship God and to enjoy His presence for ever, and they are eager to learn all they can about the God with whom they expect to spend eternity.

In this world where men forget us, change their attitude toward us as their private interests dictate, and revise their opinion of us for the slightest cause, is it not a source of wondrous strength to know that the God with whom we have to do changes not? That His attitude toward us now is the same as it was in eternity past and will be in eternity to come?

What peace it brings to the Christian's heart to realise that our Heavenly Father never differs from Himself. In coming to Him at any time we need not wonder whether we shall find Him in a receptive mood. He is always receptive to misery and need, as well as to love and faith. He does not keep office hours nor set aside periods when He will see no one. Neither does He change His mind about anything. Today, this moment, He feels toward His creatures, toward babies, toward the sick, the fallen, the sinful, exactly as He did when He sent His only begotten

Son into the world to die for mankind.

God never changes moods or cools off in His affections or loses enthusiasm. His attitude toward sin is now the same as it was when He drove out the sinful man from the eastward garden, and His attitude toward the sinner the same as when He stretched forth His hand and cried, 'Come unto me, all ye that labour and are heavy laden, and I will give you rest.'[5]

God will not compromise and He need not be coaxed. He cannot be persuaded to alter His Word nor talked into answering selfish prayer. In all our efforts to find God, to please Him, to commune with Him, we should remember that all change must be on our part. 'I am the Lord, I change not.'[6] We have but to meet His clearly stated terms, bring our lives into accord with His revealed will, and His infinite power will become instantly operative toward us in the manner set forth through the gospel in the Scriptures of truth.

Fountain of being! Source of Good!
  Immutable Thou dost remain!
Nor can the shadow of a change
  Obscure the glories of Thy reign.

Earth may with all her powers dissolve,
  If such the great Creator will;
But Thou for ever art the same,
  I AM is Thy memorial still.

From *Walker's Collection*

Notes

1 St Anselm, *op. cit.* pp.24–25.
2 2 Cor. 3:18.
3 Col. 3:10.
4 Heb. 10:9.
5 Matt. 11:28.
6 Mal. 3:6.

10

The Divine Omniscience

Lord, Thou knowest all things; Thou knowest my down-sitting and mine uprising and art acquainted with all my ways. I can inform Thee of nothing and it is vain to try to hide anything from Thee. In the light of Thy perfect knowledge I would be as artless as a little child. Help me to put away all care, for Thou knowest the way that I take and when Thou hast tried me I shall come forth as gold. Amen.

To say that God is omniscient is to say that He possesses perfect knowledge and therefore has no need to learn. But it is more: it is to say that God has never learned and cannot learn.

The Scriptures teach that God has never learned from anyone. 'Who hath directed the Spirit of the Lord, or being his counsellor hath taught him? With whom took he counsel, and who instructed him, and taught him in the path of judgment, and taught him knowledge, and shewed to him the way of understanding?'[1] 'For who hath known the mind of the Lord? Or who hath been his counsellor?'[2] These rhetorical questions put by the prophet Isaiah and the apostle Paul declare that God has never learned.

From there it is only a step to the conclusion that God cannot learn. Could God at any time or in any manner receive into His mind knowledge that He did not possess and had not possessed from eternity, He would be imperfect and less than Himself. To think of a God who must sit at the feet of a teacher, even though that teacher be an archangel or a seraph, is to think of someone other than the Most High God, maker of heaven and earth.

This negative approach to the divine omniscience is, I believe, quite justified in the circumstances. Since our intellectual knowledge of God is so small and obscure, we can sometimes gain considerable advantage in our struggle to understand what God is like by the simple expedient of thinking what He is *not* like. So far in this examination of the attributes of God we have been driven to the free use of negatives. We have seen that God had no origin, that He had no beginning, that He requires no helpers, that He suffers no change, and that in His essential being there are no limitations.

This method of trying to make men see what God is like by showing them what He is not like is used also by the inspired writers in the Holy Scriptures. 'Hast thou not known? hast thou not heard,' cries Isaiah, 'that the everlasting God, the Lord, the Creator of the ends of the earth, fainteth not, neither is weary?'[3] And that abrupt statement by God Himself, 'I am the Lord, I change not,'[4] tells us more about the divine omniscience than could be told in a ten-thousand word treatise, were all negatives arbitrarily ruled out. God's eternal truthfulness is stated negatively by the apostle Paul, 'God...cannot lie',[5] and when the angel asserted that 'with God nothing shall be impossible',[6] the two negatives add up to a ringing positive.

That God is omniscient is not only taught in the Scriptures, it must be inferred also from all else that is taught concerning Him. God perfectly knows Himself and, being the source and author of all things, it follows that He knows all that can be known. And this He knows instantly and with a fullness of perfection that includes every possible item of knowledge concerning everything that exists or could have existed anywhere in the universe at any time in the past or that may exist in the centuries or ages yet unborn.

God knows instantly and effortlessly all matter and all matters, all mind and every mind, all spirit and all spirits, all being and every being, all creaturehood and all creatures, every plurality and all pluralities, all law and every law, all relations, all causes, all thoughts, all mysteries, all enigmas, all feeling, all desires, every unuttered secret, all thrones and dominions, all personalities, all things visible and invisible in heaven and in earth, motion, space, time, life, death, good, evil, heaven, and hell.

Because God knows all things perfectly. He knows no thing better than any other thing, but all things equally well. He never discovers anything. He is never surprised, never amazed. He never wonders about anything nor (except when drawing men out for their own good) does He seek information or ask questions.

God is self-existent and self-contained and knows what no creature can ever know – Himself, perfectly.

> The things of God knoweth no man, but the Spirit of God.[7]

Only the Infinite can know the Infinite.

In the divine omniscience we see set forth against each other the terror and fascination of the Godhead. That God knows each person through and through can be a cause of shaking fear to the man that has something to hide – some unforsaken sin, some secret crime committed against man or God. The unblessed soul may well tremble that God knows the flimsiness of every pretext and never accepts the poor excuses given for sinful conduct, since He knows perfectly the real reason for it.

> Thou hast set our iniquities before thee, our secret sins in the light of thy countenance.[8]

How frightful a thing to see the sons of Adam seeking to hide among the trees of another garden. But where shall they hide?

> Whither shall I go from thy spirit? or whither shall I flee from thy presence? . . . If I say, Surely the darkness shall cover me; even the night shall be light about me. Yea, the darkness hideth not from thee; but the night shineth as the day.[9]

And to us who have fled for refuge to lay hold upon the hope that is set before us in the gospel, how unutterably sweet is the knowledge that our Heavenly Father knows us completely. No talebearer can inform on us, no enemy can make an accusation stick; no forgotten skeleton can come tumbling out of some hidden closet to abash us and expose our past; no unsuspected weakness in our characters can come to light to turn God away from us, since He knew us utterly before we knew Him and called us to Himself in the full knowledge of everything that was against us.

> For the mountains shall depart, and the hills be removed; but my kindness shall not depart from thee, neither shall the covenant of my peace be removed, saith the Lord that hath mercy on thee.[10]

Our Father in heaven knows our frame and remembers that we are dust. He knew our inborn treachery, and for His own sake engaged to save us (Is. 48:8–11). His only begotten Son, when He walked among us, felt our pains in their naked intensity of anguish. His knowledge of our afflictions and adversities is more than theoretic; it is personal, warm, and compassionate. Whatever may befall us, God knows and cares as no one else can.

> He doth give His joy to all;
> He becomes an infant small;

He becomes a man of woe;
He doth feel the sorrow too.

Think not thou canst sigh a sigh
And thy Maker is not by;
Think not thou canst weep a tear
And thy Maker is not near.

O! He gives to us His joy
That our griefs He may destroy;
Till our grief is fled and gone
He doth sit by us and moan.

William Blake

Notes

1 Isa. 40:13–14.
2 Rom. 11:34.
3 Isa. 40:28.
4 Mal. 3:6.
5 Tit. 1:2.
6 Luke 1:37.
7 1 Cor. 2:11.
8 Ps. 90:8.
9 Ps. 139:7, 11–12.
10 Isa. 54:10.

11

The Wisdom of God

Thou, O Christ, who wert tempted in all points like as we are, yet without sin, make us strong to overcome the desire to be wise and to be reputed wise by others as ignorant as ourselves. We turn from our wisdom as well as from our folly and flee to Thee, the wisdom of God and the power of God. Amen.

In this brief study of the divine wisdom we begin with faith in God. Following our usual pattern, we shall not seek to understand in order that we may believe, but to believe in order that we may understand. Hence, we shall not seek for proof that God is wise. The unbelieving mind would not be convinced by any proof, and the worshipping heart needs none.

'Blessed be the name of God for ever and ever,' cried Daniel the prophet, 'for wisdom and might are his:... he giveth wisdom unto the wise, and knowledge to them that know understanding: he revealeth the deep and secret things: he knoweth what is in the darkness, and the light dwelleth with him.'[1] The believing man responds to this, and to the angelic chant, 'Blessing, and glory, and wisdom, and thanskgiving, and honour, and power, and might, be unto our God for ever and ever.'[2] It never occurs to such a man that God should furnish proof of His wisdom or His power. Is it not enough that He is God?

When Christian theology declares that God is wise, it means vastly more than it says or can say, for it tries to make a comparatively weak word bear an incomprehensible plenitude of meaning that threatens to tear it apart and crush it under the sheer weight of the idea. 'His understanding is infinite,'[3] says the psalmist. It is nothing less than infinitude that theology is here labouring to express.

Since the word *infinite* describes what is unique, it can have no modifiers. We do not say 'more unique' or 'very infinite'. Before infinitude we stand silent.

There is indeed a secondary, created wisdom which God has given in measure to His creatures as their highest good may require; but the wisdom of any creature or of all creatures, when set against the boundless wisdom of God, is pathetically small. For this reason the apostle is accurate when he refers to God as 'only wise'.[4] That is, God is wise in Himself, and all the shining wisdom of men or angels is but a reflection of that uncreated effulgence which streams from the throne of the Majesty in the heavens.

The idea of God as infinitely wise is at the root of all truth. It is a datum of belief necessary to the soundness of all other beliefs about God. Being what He is without regard to creatures, God is of course unaffected by our opinions of Him, but our moral sanity requires that we attribute to the maker and sustainer of the universe a wisdom entirely perfect. To refuse to do this is to betray the very thing in us that distinguishes us from the beasts.

In the Holy Scriptures wisdom, when used of God and good men, always carries a strong moral connotation. It is conceived as being pure, loving, and good. Wisdom that is mere shrewdness is often attributed to evil men, but such wisdom is treacherous and false. These two kinds of wisdom are in perpetual conflict. Indeed, when seen from the lofty peak of Sinai or Calvary, the whole history of the world is discovered to be but a contest between the wisdom of God and the cunning of Satan and fallen men. The outcome of the contest is not in doubt. The imperfect must fall before the perfect at last. God has warned that He will take the wise in their own craftiness and bring to nothing the understanding of the prudent.

Wisdom, among other things, is the ability to devise perfect ends and to achieve those ends by the most perfect means. It sees the end from the beginning, so there can be no need to guess or conjecture. Wisdom sees everything in focus, each in proper relation to all, and is thus able to work toward predestined goals with flawless precision.

All God's acts are done in perfect wisdom, first for His own glory and then for the highest good of the greatest number for the longest time. And all His acts are as pure as they are wise, and as good as they are wise and pure. Not only could His acts not be better done: a better way to do them could not be imagined. An infinitely wise God must work in a manner not to be improved upon by finite creatures. O Lord, how manifold are Thy works! In wisdom hast Thou made them all. The earth is full of Thy riches!

Without the creation, the wisdom of God would have remained for ever locked in the boundless abyss of the divine nature. God brought His creatures into being that He might enjoy them and they rejoice in Him.

> And God saw everything that he had made, and, behold, it was very good.[5]

Many through the centuries have declared themselves unable to believe in the basic wisdom of a world wherein so much appears to be so wrong. Voltaire in his *Candide* introduces a determine doptimist, whom he calls Dr Pangloss, and into his mouth puts all the arguments for the 'best-of-all-possible-worlds' philosophy. Of course the French cynic took keen delight in placing the old professor insituations that made his philosophy look ridiculous.

But the Christian view of life is altogether more realistic than that of Dr Pangloss with his 'sufficient reason'. It is that this is *not* at the moment the best of all possible worlds, but one lying under the shadow of a huge calamity, the Fall of man. The inspired writers insist that the whole creation now groans and travails under the mighty shock of the Fall. They do not attempt to supply 'sufficient reasons'; they assert that the 'creature was made subject to vanity, not willingly, but by reason of him who hath subjected the same in hope'.[6] No effort here to justify the ways of God with men; just a simple declaration of fact. The being of God is its own defence.

But there is hope in all our tears. When the hour of Christ's triumph arrives, the suffering world will be brought out into the glorious liberty of the sons of God. For men of the new creation the golden age is not past but future, and when it is ushered in, a wondering universe will see that God has indeed abounded toward us in all wisdom and prudence. In the meantime we rest our hope in the only wise God, our Saviour, and wait with patience the slow development of His benign purposes.

In spite of tears and pain and death we believe that the God who made us all is infinitely wise and good. As Abraham staggered not a the promises of God through unbelief, but was strong in faith, giving glory to God, and was fully persuaded that what He had promised He was able to perform, so do we base our hope in God alone and hope against hope till the day breaks. We rest in *what God is*. I believe that this alone is true faith. Any faith that must be supported by the evidence of the senses is not real faith.

> Jesus saith unto him, Thomas, because thou hast seen me, thou hast believed: blessed are they that have not seen, and yet have believed.[7]

The testimony of faith is that, no matter how things look in this fallen world, all God's acts are wrought in perfect wisdom. The incarnation of the Eternal Son in human flesh was one of God's mighty deeds, and we may be sure that this awesome deed was done with a perfection possible only to the Infinite.

> Without controversy great is the mystery of godliness: God was manifest in the flesh.[8]

Atonement too was accomplished with the same flawless skill that marks all of God's acts. However little we understand it all, we know that Christ's expiatory work perfectly reconciled God and men and opened the kingdom of heaven to all believers. Our concern is not to explain but to proclaim. Indeed I wonder whether God could make us understand all that happened there at the cross. According to the apostle Peter not even angels know, however eagerly they may desire to look into these things.

The operation of the gospel, the new birth, the coming of the divine Spirit into human nature, the ultimate overthrow of evil, and the final establishment of Christ's righteous kingdom – all these have flowed and do flow out of God's infinite fullness of wisdom. The sharpest eyes of the holiest watcher in the blest company above cannot discover a flaw in the ways of God in bringing all this to fruition, nor can the pooled wisdom of seraphim and cherubim suggest how an improvement might be made in the divine procedure.

> I know that, whatsoever God doeth, it shall be for ever: nothing can be put to it, nor any thing taken from it: and God doeth it, that men should fear before him.[9]

It is vitally important that we hold the truth of God's infinite wisdom as a tenet of our creed; but this is not enough. We must by the exercise of faith and by prayer bring it into the practical world of our day-by-day experience.

To believe actively that our Heavenly Father constantly spreads around us providential circumstances that work for our present good and our everlasting well-being brings to the soul a veritable benediction. Most of us go through life praying a little, planning a little, jockeying for position, hoping but never being quite certain of anything, and always secretly afraid that we will miss the way. This is a tragic waste of truth and never gives rest to the heart.

There is a better way. It is to repudiate our own wisdom and take instead the infinite wisdom of God. Our insistence upon seeing ahead is natural enough, but it is a real hindrance to our spiritual progress. God has charged Himself with full responsibility for our eternal happiness and stands ready to take over the management of our lives the moment we turn in faith to Him. Here is His promise:

> And I will bring the blind by a way that they knew not; I will lead them in paths that they have not known: I will make darkness light before them, and crooked things straight. These things will I do unto them, and not forsake them.[10]

> Let Him lead thee blindfold onwards,
> Love needs not to know;
> Children whom the Father leadeth
> Ask not where they go.
> Though the path be all unknown,
> Over moors and mountains lone.
>
> *Gerhard Tersteegen*

God constantly encourages us to trust Him in the dark.

> I will go before thee, and make the crooked places straight: I will break in pieces the gates of brass, and cut in sunder the bars of iron; and I will give thee the treasures of darkness, and the hidden riches of secret places, that thou mayest know that I, the Lord, which call thee by thy name, am the God of Israel.[11]

It is heartening to learn how many of God's mighty deeds were done in secret, away from the prying eyes of men or angels. When God created the heavens and the earth, darkness was upon the face of the deep. When the Eternal Son became flesh, He was carried for a time in the darkness of the sweet virgin's womb. When He died for the life of the world, it was in the darkness, seen by no one at the last. When He arose from the dead, it was 'very early in the morning'.[12] No one saw Him rise. It is as if God were saying, 'What I am is all that need matter to you, for there lie your hope and your peace. I will do what I will do, and it will all come to light at last, but how I do it is My secret. Trust Me, and be not afraid.'

With the goodness of God to desire our highest welfare, the wisdom of God to plan it, and the power of God to achieve it, what do we lack? Surely we are the most favoured of all creatures.

> In all our Maker's grand designs,
> Omnipotence, with wisdom, shines;
> His works, through all this wondrous frame,
> Declare the glory of His Name.
>
> *Thomas Blacklock*

Notes

1 Dan. 2:20–22.
2 Rev. 7:12.

3 Ps. 147:5.
4 1 Tim. 1:17.
5 Gen. 1:31.
6 Rom. 8:20.
7 John 20:29.
8 1 Tim. 3:16.
9 Eccles. 3:14.
10 Isa. 42:16.
11 Isa. 45:2–3.
12 Luke 24:1.

12

The Omnipotence of God

Our Heavenly Father, we have heard Thee say, 'I am the Almighty God; walk before me, and be thou perfect.' But unless Thou dost enable us by the exceeding greatness of Thy power how can we who are by nature weak and sinful walk in a perfect way? Grant that we may learn to lay hold on the working of the mighty power which wrought in Christ when Thou didst raise Him from the dead and set Him at Thine own right hand in the heavenly places. Amen.

In the time of his vision John the revelator heard as it were the voice of a great multitude and as the voice of many waters and as the voice of mighty thunderings sounding throughout the universe, and what the voice proclaimed was the sovereignty and omnipotence of God:

> Alleluia: for the Lord God omnipotent reigneth.[1]

Sovereignty and omnipotence must go together. One cannot exist without the other. To reign, God must have power, and to reign sovereignly, He must have all power. And that is what *omnipotent* means, having all power. The word derives from the Latin and is identical in meaning with the more familiar *almighty* which we have from the Anglo-Saxon. This latter word occurs fifty-six times in our English Bible and is never used of anyone but

God. He alone is almighty.

God possesses what no creature can: an incomprehensible plenitude of power, a potency that is absolute. This we know by divine revelation, but once known, it is recognised as being in full accord with reason. Grant that God is infinite and self-existent and we see at once that He must be all-powerful as well, and reason kneels to worship before the divine omnipotence.

'Power belongeth unto God,'[2] says the psalmist, and Paul the apostle declares that nature itself gives evidence of the eternal power of the Godhead (Rom. 1:20). From this knowledge we reason to the omnipotence of God this way: God has power. Since God is also infinite, whatever He has must be without limit; therefore God has limitless power, He is omnipotent. We see further that God the self-existent Creator is the source of all the power there is, and since a source must be at least equal to anything that emanates from it, God is of necessity equal to all the power there is, and this is to say again that He is omnipotent.

God has delegated power to His creatures, but being self-sufficient, He cannot relinquish anything of His perfections and, power being one of them, He has never surrendered the least iota of His power. He gives but He does not give away. All that He gives remains His own and returns to Him again. For ever He must remain what He has for ever been, the Lord God omnipotent.

One cannot long read the Scriptures sympathetically without noticing the radical disparity between the outlook of men of the Bible and that of modern men. We are today suffering from a secularised mentality. Where the sacred writers saw God, we see the laws of nature. Their world was fully populated; ours is all but empty. Their world was alive and personal; ours is impersonal and dead. God ruled their world; ours is ruled by the laws of nature and we are always once removed from the presence of God.

And what are these laws of nature that have displaced God in the minds of millions? Law has two meanings. One is an external rule enforced by authority, such as the common rule against robbery and assault. The word is also used to denote the uniform way things act in the universe, but this second use of the word is erroneous. What we see in nature is simply the paths God's power and wisdom take through creation. Properly these are phenomena, not laws, but we call them laws by analogy with the arbitrary laws of society.

Science observes how the power of God operates, discovers a regular pattern somewhere and fixes it as a 'law'. The uniformity of God's activities in His creation enables the scientist to predict the course of natural phenomena. The trustworthiness of God's behaviour in His world is the foundation of all scientific truth. Upon it the scientist rests his faith and from there he goes on to achieve great and useful things in such fields as those of navigation, chemistry, agriculture, and the medical arts.

Religion, on the other hand, goes behind nature to God. It is concerned not with the footprints of God along the paths of creation, but with the One who treads those paths. Religion is interested primarily in the One who is the source of all things, the master of every phenomenon. For this One philosophy has various names, the most horrendous that I have seen being that supplied by Rudolf Otto: 'The absolute, the gigantic, never-resting, active world stress.'[3] The Christian delights to remember that this 'world stress' once said 'I AM',[4] and that the greatest teacher of them all directed His disciples to address Him as a person: 'When ye pray, say, Our Father which art in heaven, Hallowed be thy name.'[5] The men of the Bible everywhere communed with this 'gigantic absolute' in language as personal as speech affords, and with Him prophet and saint walked in a rapture of devotion, warm, intimate, and deeply satisfying.

Omnipotence is not a name given to the sum of all power, but an attribute of a personal God whom we Christians believe to be the Father of our Lord Jesus Christ and of all who believe on Him to life eternal. The worshipping man finds this knowledge a source of wonderful strength for his inner life. His faith rises to take the great leap upward into the fellowship of Him who can do whatever He wills to do, for whom nothing is hard or difficult because He possesses power absolute.

Since He has at His command all the power in the universe, the Lord God omnipotent can do anything as easily as anything else. All His acts are done without effort. He expends no energy that must be replenished. His self-sufficiency makes it unnecessary for Him to look outside of Himself for a renewal of strength. All the power required to do all that He wills to do lies in undiminished fullness in His own infinite being.

The Presbyterian pastor, A. B. Simpson, approaching middle age, broken in health, deeply despondent and ready to quit the ministry, chanced to hear the simple Negro spiritual,

> Nothing is too hard for Jesus,
> No man can work like Him.

Its message sped like an arrow to his heart, carrying faith and hope and life for body and soul. He sought a place of retirement and after a season alone with God arose to his feet completely cured, and went forth in fullness of joy to found what has since become one of the largest foreign missionary societies in the world. For thirty-five years after this encounter with God, he laboured prodigiously in the service of Christ. His faith in the God of limitless power gave him all the strength he needed to carry on.

Almighty One! I bend in dust before Thee;
Even so veiled cherubs bend;
In calm and still devotion I adore Thee,
All-wise, all-present Friend.

Thou to the earth its emerald robe hast given,
Or curtained it in snow;
And the bright sun, and the soft moon in heaven,
Before Thy presence bow.

Sir John Bowring

Notes

1 Rev. 19:6.
2 Ps. 62:11.
3 Rudolf Otto, *The Idea of the Holy* (Oxford University Press, New York, 1958) p.24.
4 Ex. 3:14.
5 Luke 11:2.

13

The Divine Transcendence

O Lord our Lord, there is none like Thee in heaven above or in the earth beneath. Thine is the greatness and the dignity and the majesty. All that is in the heaven and the earth is Thine; Thine is the kingdom and the power and the glory for ever, O God, and Thou art exalted as head over all. Amen.

When we speak of God as transcendent we mean of course that He is exalted far above the created universe, so far above that human thought cannot imagine it.

To think accurately about this, however, we must keep in mind that 'far above' does not here refer to physical distance from the earth but to quality of being. We are concerned not with location in space nor with mere altitude, but with life.

God is spirit, and to Him magnitude and distance have no meaning. To us they are useful as analogies and illustrations, so God refers to them constantly when speaking down to our limited understanding. The words of God as found in Isaiah, 'Thus saith the high and lofty One that inhabiteth eternity,'[1] give a distinct impression of altitude, but that is because we who dwell in a world of matter, space, and time tend to think in material terms and can grasp abstract ideas only when they are identified in some way with material things. In its struggle to free itself from the tyranny of the natural world, the human heart must learn to translate upward the language the Spirit uses to instruct us.

It is spirit that gives significance to matter and apart from spirit nothing has any value at last. A little child strays from a party of sightseers and becomes lost on a mountain, and immediately the whole mental perspective of the members of the party is changed. Rapt admiration for the grandeur of nature gives way to acute distress for the lost child. The group spreads out over the mountain-side anxiously calling the child's name and searching eagerly into every secluded spot where the little one might chance to be hidden.

What brought about this sudden change? The tree-clad mountain is still there towering into the clouds in breath-taking beauty, but no one notices it now. All attention is focused upon the search for a curly-haired little girl not yet two years old and weighing less than thirty pounds. Though so new and so small, she is more precious to parents and friends than all the huge bulk of the vast and ancient mountain they had been admiring a few minutes before. And in their judgement the whole civilised world concurs, for the little girl can love and laugh and speak and pray, and the mountain cannot. It is the child's quality of being that gives it worth.

Yet we must not compare the being of God with any other as we just now compared the mountain with the child. We must not think of God as highest in an ascending order of beings, starting with the single cell and going on up from the fish to the bird to the animal to man to angel to cherub to God. This would be to grant God eminence, even pre-eminence, but that is not enough; we must grant Him *transcendence* in the fullest meaning of that word. For ever God stands apart, in light unapproachable. He is as high above an archangel as above a caterpillar, for the gulf that separates the archangel from the caterpillar is but finite, while the gulf between God and the archangel is infinite. The caterpillar and the archangel, though far removed from each other in the scale of created things, are nevertheless one in that they are alike created. They both belong in the category of that-which-is-not God and are separated from God by infinitude itself.

Reticence and compulsion for ever contend within the heart that would speak of God.

> How shall polluted mortals dare
> To sing Thy glory or Thy grace?
> Beneath Thy feet we lie afar,
> And see but shadows of Thy face.
> *Isaac Watts*

Yet we console ourselves with the knowledge that it is God Himself who puts it in our hearts to seek Him and makes it possible in some measure to know Him, and He is pleased with even the feeblest effort to make Him known.

If some watcher or holy one who has spent his glad centuries by the sea of fire were to come to earth, how meaningless to him would be the ceaseless chatter of the busy tribes of men. How strange to him and how empty would sound the flat, stale and profitless words heard in the average pulpit from week to week. And were such a one to speak on earth would he not speak of God? Would he not charm and fascinate his hearers with rapturous descriptions of the Godhead? And after hearing him could we ever again consent to listen to anything less than theology, the doctrine of God? Would we not therefore demand of those who would presume to teach us that they speak to us from the mount of divine vision or remain silent altogether?

When the psalmist saw the transgression of the wicked his heart told him how it could be. 'There is no fear of God before his eyes,'[2] he explained, and in so saying revealed to us the psychology of sin. When men no longer fear God, they transgress His laws without hestitation. The fear of consequences is no deterrent when the fear of God is gone.

In olden days men of faith were said to 'walk in the fear of God' and to 'serve the Lord with fear'. However intimate their communion with God, however bold their prayers, at the base of their religious life was the conception of God as awesome and dreadful. This idea of God transcendent runs through the whole Bible and gives colour and tone to the character of the saints. This fear of God was more than a natural apprehension of danger; it was a non-rational dread, an acute feeling of personal insufficiency in the presence of God the Almighty.

Wherever God appeared to men in Bible times the results were the same – an overwhelming sense of terror and dismay, a wrenching sensation of sinfulness and guilt. When God spoke, Abram stretched himself upon the ground to listen. When Moses saw the Lord in the burning bush, he hid his face in fear to look upon God. Isaiah's vision of God wrung from him the cry, 'Woe is me!' and the confession, 'I am undone; because I am a man of unclean lips.'[3]

Daniel's encounter with God was probably the most dreadful and wonderful of them all. The prophet lifted up his eyes and saw One whose 'body was also like the beryl, and his face as the appearance of lightning, and his eyes as lamps of fire, and his arms and his feet like in colour to polished brass, and the voice of his words like the voice of a multitude.' 'I Daniel alone saw the vision,' he afterwards wrote, 'For the men that were with me saw not the vision; but a great quaking fell upon them, so that they fled to hide themselves. Therefore I was left alone, and saw this great vision, and there remained no strength in me: for my comeliness was turned in me into corruption, and I retained no strength. Yet heard I the voice of his words: and when I heard the voice of his words, then was I in a deep sleep on my face, and my face toward the ground.'[4]

These experiences show that a vision of the divine transcendence soon ends all controversy between the man and his God. The fight goes out of the man and he is ready with the conquered Saul to ask meekly, 'Lord, what wilt thou have me to do?'[5] Conversely, the self-assurance of modern Christians, the basic levity present in so many of our religious gatherings, the shocking disrespect shown for the person of God, are evidence enough of deep blindness of heart. Many call themselves by the name of Christ, talk much about God, and pray to Him sometimes, but evidently do not know who He is. 'The fear of the Lord is a fountain of life,'[6] but this healing fear is today hardly found among Christian men.

Once in conversation with his friend Eckermann, the poet Goethe turned to thoughts of religion and spoke of the abuse of the divine name. 'People treat it,' he said, 'as if that incomprehensible and most high Being, who is even beyond the reach of thought, were only their equal. Otherwise they would not say "the Lord God, the dear God, the good God". This expression becomes to them, especially to the clergy, who have it daily in their mouths, a mere phrase, a barren name, to which no thought whatever is attached. If they were impressed by His greatness they would be dumb, and through veneration unwilling to name Him.'[7]

Lord of all being, throned afar,
Thy glory flames from sun and star;
Centre and soul of every sphere,
Yet to each loving heart how near!

Lord of all life, below, above,
Whose light is truth, whose warmth is love,
Before Thy ever-blazing throne
We ask no lustre of our own.

Oliver Wendell Holmes

Notes

1 Isa. 57:15.
2 Ps. 36:1.
3 Isa. 6:5.
4 Dan. 10:6–9.
5 Acts 9:6.
6 Prov. 14:27.
7 Johann Peter Eckermann, *Conversations with Eckermann* (M. Walter Dunn, Washington and London, 1901) p.45.

14

God's Omnipresence

Our Father, we know that Thou art present with us, but our knowledge is but a figure and shadow of truth and has little of the spiritual savour and inward sweetness such knowledge should afford. This is for us a great loss and the cause of much weakness of heart. Help us to make at once such amendment of life as is necessary before we can experience the true meaning of the words 'In thy presence is fullness of joy.' Amen.

The word present, of course, means *here, close to, next to,* and the prefix *omni* gives it universality. God is everywhere here, close to everything, next to everyone.

Few other truths are taught in the Scriptures with as great clarity as the doctrine of the divine omnipresence. Those passages supporting this truth are so plain that it would take considerable effort to misunderstand them. They declare that God is immanent in His creation, that there is no place in heaven or earth or hell where men may hide from His presence. They teach that God is at once far off and near, and that in Him men move and live and have their being. And what is equally convincing is that they everywhere compel us to assume that God is omnipresent to account for other facts they tell us about Him.

For instance, the Scriptures teach that God is infinite. This means that His being knows no limits. Therefore there can be no limit to His presence; He is omnipresent. In His infinitude He surrounds the finite creation and contains it. There is no place beyond Him for anything to be. God is our environment as the sea is to the fish and the air to the bird. 'God is over all things,' wrote Hildebert of Lavardin, 'under all things; outside all; within but not enclosed; without but not excluded; above but not raised up; below but not depressed; wholly above, presiding; wholly beneath, sustaining; wholly within, filling.'[1]

The belief that God is present within His universe cannot be held in isolation. It has practical implications in many areas of theological thought and bears directly upon certain religious problems, such as, for instance, the nature of the world. Thinking men of almost every age and culture have been concerned with the question of what kind of world this is. Is it a material world running by itself, or is it spiritual and run by unseen powers? Does this interlocking system explain itself or does its secret lie in mystery? Does the stream of existence begin and end in itself? Or is its source higher up and father back than the hills?

Christian theology claims to have the answer to these questions. It does not speculate nor offer an opinion but presents its 'Thus saith the Lord' as its authority. It declares positively that the world is spiritual: it originated in spirit, flows out of spirit, is spiritual in its essence, and is meaningless apart from the Spirit that inhabits it.

The doctrine of the divine omnipresence personalises man's relation to the universe in which he finds himself. This great central truth gives meaning to all other truths and imparts supreme value to all his little life. God is present, near him, next to him, and this God sees him and knows him through and through. At this point faith begins, and while it may go on to include a thousand other wonderful truths, these all refer back to the truth that *God is, and God is here*. 'He that cometh to God,' says the book of Hebrews, 'must believe that he is.'[2] And Christ Himself said, 'Ye believe in God, believe also....'[3] Whatever 'also' may be added to the elementary belief in God is superstructure, and regardless of the heights to which it may rise, it continues to rest solidly upon the original foundation.

The teaching of the New Testament is that God created the world by the *Logos*, the Word, and the Word is identified with the second person of the Godhead who was present in the world even before He became incarnate in human nature. The Word made all things and remained in His creation to uphold and sustain it and be at the same time a moral light enabling every man to distinguish good from evil. The universe operates as an orderly system, not by impersonal laws but by the creative voice of the immanent and universal presence, the *Logos*.

Canon W. G. H. Holmes of India told of seeing Hindu worshippers tapping on trees and stones and whispering 'Are you there? Are you there?' to the god they hoped might reside within. In complete humility the instructed Christian brings the answer to that question. God is indeed there. He is there as He is here and everywhere, not confined to tree or stone, but free in the universe, near to everything, next to everyone, and through Jesus Christ immediately accessible to every loving heart. The doctrine of the divine omnipresence decides this for ever.

This truth is to the convinced Christian a source of deep comfort in sorrow and of steadfast assurance in all the varied experiences of his life. To him 'the practice of the presence of God' consists not of projecting an imaginary object from within his own mind and then seeking to realise its presence; it is rather to recognise the real presence of the One whom all sound theology declares to be already there, an objective entity, existing apart from any apprehension of Him on the part of His creatures. The resultant experience is not visionary but real.

The certainty that God is always near us, present in all parts of His world, closer to us than our thoughts, should maintain us in a state of high moral happiness most of the time. But not all the time. It would be less than honest to promise every believer continual jubilee and less than realistic to expect it. As a child may cry out in pain even when sheltered in its mother's arms, so a Christian may sometimes know what it is to suffer even in the conscious presence of God. Though 'alway rejoicing',[4] Paul admitted that he was sometimes sorrowful, and for our sakes Christ experienced strong crying and tears though He never left the bosom of the Father (John 1:18).

But all will be well. In a world like this tears have their therapeutic effects. The healing balm distilled from the garments of the enfolding presence cures our ills before they become fatal. The knowledge that we are never alone calms the troubled sea of our lives and speaks peace to our souls.

That God is here both Scripture and reason declare. It remains only for us to learn to realise this in conscious experience. A sentence from a letter by Dr Allen Fleece sums up the testimony of many others: 'The knowledge that God is present is blessed, but to *feel* His presence is nothing less than sheer happiness.

God reveals His presence:
Let us now adore Him,
And with awe appear before Him.

Him alone, God we own;
He's our Lord and Saviour,
Praise His name for ever.

God Himself is with us:
Whom the angelic legions
Serve with awe in heavenly regions.

Gerhard Tersteegen

Notes

1 *A New Dictionary of Quotations*, selected and edited by H. L. Mencken (Alfred A. Knopf, New York, 1942) pp.462–463.
2 Heb. 11:6.
3 John 14:1.
4 2 Cor. 6:10.

15

The Faithfulness of God

It is a good thing to give thanks unto Thee and to sing praises unto Thy name, O Most High, to show forth Thy loving-kindness in the morning and Thy faithfulness every night. As Thy Son while on earth was loyal to Thee, His Heavenly Father, so now in heaven He is faithful to us, His earthly brethren: and in this knowledge we press on with every confident hope for all the years and centuries yet to come. Amen.

As emphasised earlier, God's attributes are not isolated traits of His character but facets of His unitary being. They are not things-in-themselves; they are, rather, thoughts by which we think of God, aspects of a perfect whole, names given to whatever we know to be true of the Godhead.

To have a correct understanding of the attributes it is necessary that we see them all as one. We can think of them separately but they cannot be separated. 'All attributes assigned to God cannot differ in reality, by reason of the perfect simplicity of God, although we in divers ways use of God divers words,' says Nicholas of Cusa. 'Whence, although we attribute to God sight, hearing, taste, smell, touch, sense, reason and intellect, and so forth, according to the divers significations of each word, yet in Him sight is not other than hearing, or tasting, or smelling, or touching, or feeling, or understanding. And so all theology is said to be stablished in a circle, because any one of His attributes is affirmed of another.'[1]

In studying any attribute, the essential oneness of all the attributes soon becomes apparent. We see, for instance, that if God is self-existent He must be also self-sufficient; and if He has power He, being infinite, must have all power. If He possesses knowledge, His infinitude assures us that He possesses all knowledge. Similarly, His immutability presupposes His faithfulness. If He is unchanging, it follows that He could not be unfaithful, since that would require Him to change. Any failure within the divine character would argue imperfection and, since God is perfect, it could not occur. Thus the attributes explain each other and prove that they are but glimpses the mind enjoys of the absolutely perfect Godhead.

All of God's acts are consistent with all of His attributes. No attribute contradicts any other, but all harmonise and blend into each other in the infinite abyss of the Godhead. All that God does agrees with all that God is, and being and doing are one in Him. The familiar picture of God as often torn between His justice and His mercy is altogether false to the facts. To think of God as inclining first toward one and then toward another of His attributes is to imagine a God who is unsure of Himself, frustrated and emotionally unstable, which of course is to say that the one of whom we are thinking is not the true God at all but a weak, mental reflection of Him badly out of focus.

God, being who He is, cannot cease to be what He is, and being what He is, He cannot act out of character with Himself. He is at once faithful and immutable, so all His words and acts must be and must remain faithful. Men become unfaithful out of desire, fear, weakness, loss of interest, or because of some strong influence from without. Obviously none of these forces can affect God in any way. He is His own reason for all He is and does. He cannot be compelled from without, but ever speaks and acts from within Himself by His own sovereign will as it pleases Him.

I think it might be demonstrated that almost every heresy that has afflicted the church through the years has arisen from believing about God things that are not true, or from over-emphasising certain true things so as to obscure other things equally true. To magnify any attribute to the exclusion of another is to head straight for one of the dismal swamps of theology; and yet we are all constantly tempted to do just that.

For instance, the Bible teaches that God is love; some have interpreted this in such a way as virtually to deny that He is just, which the Bible also teaches. Others press the biblical doctrine of God's goodness so far that it is made to contradict His holiness. Or they make His compassion cancel out His truth. Still others understand the sovereignty of God in a way that destroys or at least greatly diminishes His goodness and love.

We can hold a correct view of truth only by daring to believe everything God has said about Himself. It is a grave responsibility that a man takes upon himself when he seeks to edit out of God's self-revelation such features as he in his ignorance deems objectionable. Blindness in part must surely fall upon any of us presumptuous enough to attempt such a thing. And it is wholly uncalled for. We need not fear to let the truth stand as it is written. There is no conflict among the divine attributes. God's being is unitary. He cannot divide Himself and act at a given time from one of His attributes while the rest remain inactive. All that God is must accord with all that God does. Justice must be present in mercy, and love in judgement. And so with all the divine attributes.

The faithfulness of God is a datum of sound theology but to the believer it becomes far more than that: it passes through the processes of the understanding and goes on to become nourishing food for the soul. For the Scriptures not only teach truth, they show also its uses for mankind. The inspired writers were men of like passion with us, dwelling in the midst of life. What they learned about God became to them a sword, a shield, a hammer; it became their life motivation, their good hope, and their confident expectation. From the objective facts of theology their hearts made how many thousand joyous deductions and personal applications! The book of Psalms rings with glad thanksgiving for the faithfulness of God. The New Testament takes up the theme and celebrates the loyalty of God the Father and His Son Jesus Christ who before Pontius Pilate witnessed a good confession; and in the Apocalypse Christ is seen astride a white horse riding toward His triumph, and the names He bears are Faithful and True.

Christian song, too, celebrates the attributes of God, and among them the divine faithfulness. In our hymnody, at its best, the attributes become the wellspring from which flow rivers of joyous melody. Some old hymnbooks may yet be found in which the hymns have no names; a line in italics above each one indicates its theme, and the worshipping heart cannot but rejoice in what it finds: '*God's glorious perfections celebrated.*' '*Wisdom, majesty and goodness.*' '*Omniscience.*' '*Omnipotence and immutability.*' '*Glory, mercy and grace.*' These are a few samples taken from a hymnbook published in 1849, but everyone familiar with Christian hymnody knows that the stream of sacred song takes its rise far back in the early years of the Church's existence. From the beginning belief in the perfection of God brought sweet assurance to believing men and taught the ages to sing.

Upon God's faithfulness rests our whole hope of future

blessedness. Only as He is faithful will His covenant stand and His promises be honoured. Only as we have complete assurance that He is faithful may we live in peace and look forward with assurance to the life to come.

Every heart can make its own application of this truth and draw from it such conclusions as the truth suggests and its own needs bring into focus. The tempted, the anxious, the fearful, the discouraged may all find new hope and good cheer in the knowledge that our Heavenly Father is faithful. He will ever be true to His pledged word. The hard-pressed sons of the covenant may be sure that He will never remove His loving-kindness from them nor suffer His faithfulness to fail.

> Happy the man whose hopes rely
> On Israel's God; He made the sky,
> And earth, and seas, with all their train;
> His truth for ever stands secure;
> He saves the oppressed, He feeds the poor,
> And none shall find His promise vain.
>
> *Isaac Watts*

Notes

1 Nicholas of Cusa, *op. cit.* p.12.

16

The Goodness of God

Do good in Thy good pleasure unto us, O Lord. Act toward us not as we deserve but as it becomes Thee, being the God Thou art. So shall we have nothing to fear in this world or in that which is to come. Amen.

The word *good* means so many things to so many persons that this brief study of the divine goodness begins with a definition. The meaning may be arrived at only by the use of a number of synonyms, going out from and returning by different paths to the same place.

When Christian theology says that God is good, it is not the same as saying that He is righteous or holy. The holiness of God is trumpeted from the heavens and re-echoed on earth by saints and sages wherever God has revealed Himself to men; however, we are not at this time considering His holiness but His goodness, which is quite another thing.

The goodness of God is that which disposes Him to be kind, cordial, benevolent, and full of good will toward men. He is tender-hearted and of quick sympathy, and His unfailing attitude toward all moral beings is open, frank, and friendly. By His nature He is inclined to bestow blessedness and He takes holy pleasure in the happiness of His people.

That God is good is taught or implied on every page of the Bible and must be received as an article of faith as impregnable as the throne of God. It is a foundation stone for all sound thought about God and is necessary to moral sanity. To allow that God could be other than good is to deny the validity of all thought and end in the negation of every moral judgement. If God is not good, then there can be no distinction between kindness and cruelty, and heaven can be hell and hell, heaven.

The goodness of God is the drive behind all the blessings He daily bestows upon us. God created us because He felt good in His heart and He redeemed us for the same reason.

Julian of Norwich, who lived six hundred years ago, saw clearly that the ground of all blessedness is the goodness of God. Chapter six of her incredibly beautiful and perceptive little classic, *Revelations of Divine Love,* begins, 'This showing was made to learn our souls to cleave wisely to the goodness of God.' Then she lists some of the mighty deeds God has wrought in our behalf, and after each one she adds 'of His goodness'. She saw that all our religious activities and every means of grace, however right and useful they may be, are nothing until we understand that the unmerited, spontaneous goodness of God is behind all and underneath all His acts.

Divine goodness, as one of God's attributes, is self-caused, infinite, perfect, and eternal. Since God is immutable He never varies in the intensity of His loving-kindness. He has never been kinder than He now is, nor will He ever be less kind. He is no respecter of persons but makes His sun to shine on the evil as well as on the good, and sends His rain on the just and on the unjust. The cause of his goodness is in Himself; the recipients of His goodness are all His beneficiaries without merit and without recompense.

With this agrees reason, and the moral wisdom that knows itself runs to acknowledge that there can be no merit in human conduct, not even in the purest and the best. Always God's goodness is the ground of our expectation. Repentance, though necessary, is not meritorious but a condition for receiving the gracious gift of pardon which God gives of His goodness. Prayer is not in itself meritorious. It lays God under no obligation nor puts Him in debt to any. He hears prayer because He is good, and for no other reason. Nor is faith meritorious; it is simply confidence in the goodness of God, and the lack of it is a reflection upon God's holy character.

The whole outlook of mankind might be changed if we could all believe that we dwell under a friendly sky and that the God of heaven, though exalted in power and majesty, is eager to be friends with us.

But sin has made us timid and self-conscious, as well it might. Years of rebellion against God have bred in us a fear that cannot be overcome in a day. The captured rebel does not enter willingly the presence of the king he has so long fought unsuccessfully to overthrow. But if he is truly penitent he may come, trusting only in the loving-kindness of his Lord, and the past will not be held against him. Meister Eckhart encourages us to remember that, when we return to God, even if our sins were as great in number as all mankind's put together, still God would not count them against us, but would have as much confidence in us as if we had never sinned.

Now someone who in spite of his past sins honestly wants to become reconciled to God may cautiously inquire, 'If I come to God, how will He act toward me? What kind of disposition has He? What will I find Him to be like?'

The answer is that He will be found to be exactly like Jesus. 'He that hath seen me,' said Jesus, 'hath seen the Father.'[1] Christ walked with men on earth that He might show them what God is like and make known the true nature of God to a race that had wrong ideas about Him. This was only one of the things He did while here in the flesh, but this He did with beautiful perfection.

From Him we learn how God acts toward people. The hypocritical, the basically insincere, will find Him cold and aloof, as they once found Jesus; but the penitent will find Him merciful; the self-condemned will find Him generous and kind. To the frightened He is friendly, to the poor in spirit He is forgiving, to the ignorant, considerate; to the weak, gentle; to the stranger, hospitable.

By our own attitudes we may determine our reception by Him. Though the kindness of God is an infinite, overflowing fountain of cordiality, God will not force His attention upon us. If we would be welcomed as the prodigal was, we must come as the prodigal came; and when we so come, even though the Pharisees and the legalists sulk without, there will be a feast of welcome within, and music and dancing as the Father takes His child again to His heart.

The greatness of God rouses fear within us, but His goodness encourages us not to be afraid of Him. To fear and not be afraid – that is the paradox of faith.

O God, my hope, my heavenly rest,
My all of happiness below.
Grant my importunate request,
To me, to me, Thy goodness show;
Thy beatific face display,
The brightness of eternal day.

Before my faith's enlightened eyes,
Make all Thy gracious goodness pass;
Thy goodness is the sight I prize:
O might I see Thy smiling face:
Thy nature in my soul proclaim,
Reveal Thy love, Thy glorious name.

Charles Wesley

Notes

1 John 14:9.

17

The Justice of God

Our Father, we love Thee for Thy justice. We acknowledge that Thy judgements are true and righteous altogether. Thy justice upholds the order of the universe and guarantees the safety of all who put their trust in Thee. We live because Thou art just – and merciful. Holy, holy, holy, Lord God Almighty, righteous in all Thy ways and holy in all Thy works. Amen.

In the inspired Scriptures justice and righteousness are scarcely to be distinguished from each other. The same word in the original becomes in English *justice* or *righteousness*, almost, one would suspect, at the whim of the translator.

The Old Testament asserts God's justice in language clear and full, and as beautiful as may be found anywhere in the literature of mankind. When the destruction of Sodom was announced, Abraham interceded for the righteous within the city, reminding God that he knew He would act like Himself in the human emergency. 'That be far from thee to do after this manner, to slay the righteous with the wicked: and that the righteous should be as the wicked, that be far from thee: Shall not the Judge of all the earth do right?'[1]

The concept of God held by the psalmists and prophets of Israel was that of an all-powerful ruler, high and lifted up, reigning in equity. 'Clouds and darkness are round about him: righteousness and judgement are the habitation of his throne.'[2] Of the long-awaited Messiah it was prophesied that when He came He should judge the people with righteousness and the poor with judgement. Holy men of tender compassion, outraged by the inequity of the world's rulers, prayed, 'O Lord God, to whom vengeance belongeth; O God, to whom vengeance belongeth, shew thyself. Lift up thyself, thou judge of the earth: render a reward to the proud. Lord, how long shall the wicked, how long shall the wicked triumph?'[3] And this is to be understood not as a plea for personal vengeance but as a longing to see moral equity prevail in human society.

Such men as David and Daniel acknowledged their own unrighteousness in contrast to the righteousness of God, and as a result their penitential prayers gained great power and effectiveness. 'O Lord, righteousness belongeth unto thee, but unto us confusion of faces.'[4] And when the long-withheld judgement of God begins to fall upon the world, John sees the victorious saints standing upon a sea of glass mingled with fire. In their hands they hold the harps of God; the song they sing is the song of Moses and the Lamb, and the theme of their song is the divine justice. 'Great and marvellous are thy works, Lord God Almighty; just and true are thy ways, thou King of saints. Who shall not fear thee, O Lord, and glorify thy name? for thou alone art holy: for all nations shall come and worship before thee; for thy judgments are made manifest.'[5]

Justice embodies the idea of moral equity, and iniquity is the exact opposite; it is *in*-equity, the absence of equality from human thoughts and acts. Judgement is the application of equity to moral situations and may be favourable or unfavourable according to whether the one under examination has been equitable or inequitable in heart and conduct.

It is sometimes said, 'Justice requires God to do this,' referring to some act we know He will perform. This is an error of thinking as well as of speaking, for it postulates a principle of justice outside of God which compels Him to act in a certain way. Of course there is no such principle. If there were it would be superior to God, for only a superior power can compel obedience. The truth is that there is not and can never be anything outside of the nature of God which can move Him in the least degree. All God's reasons come from within His uncreated being. Nothing has entered the being of God from eternity, nothing has been removed, and nothing has been changed.

Justice, when used of God, is a name we give to the way God is, nothing more; and when God acts justly He is not doing so to conform to an independent criterion, but simply acting like Himself in a given situation. As gold is an element in itself and can never change nor compromise but is gold wherever it is found, so God is God, always, only, fully God, and can never be other than He is. Everything in the universe is good to the degree it conforms to the nature of God and evil as it fails to do so. God is His own self-existent principle of moral equity, and when He sentences evil men or rewards the righteous, He simply acts like Himself from within, uninfluenced by anything that is not Himself.

All this seems, but only seems, to destroy the hope of justification for the returning sinner. The Christian philosopher and saint, Anselm, Archbishop of Canterbury, sought a solution to the apparent contradiction between the justice and the mercy of God. 'How dost Thou spare the wicked,' he inquired of God, 'if Thou art all just and supremely just?'[6] Then he looked straight at God for the answer, for he knew that it lies in *what God is*. Anselm's findings may be paraphrased this way: God's being is unitary; it is not composed of a number of parts working harmoniously, but simply one. There is nothing in His justice which forbids the exercise of His mercy. To think of God as we sometimes think of a court where a kindly judge, compelled by law, sentences a man to death with tears and apologies, is to think in a manner wholly unworthy of the true God. God is never at cross-purposes with Himself. No attribute of God is in conflict with another.

God's compassion flows out of His goodness, and goodness without justice is not goodness. God spares us because He is good, but He could not be good if He were not just. When God punishes the wicked, Anselm concludes, it is just because it is consistent with their deserts; and when He spares the wicked it is just because it is compatible with His goodness; so God does what becomes Him as the supremely good God. This is reason seeking to understand, not that it may believe but because it already believes.

A simpler and more familiar solution for the problem of how God can be just and still justify the unjust is found in the Christian doctrine of redemption. It is that, through the work of Christ in atonement, justice is not violated but satisfied when God spares a sinner. Redemptive theology teaches that mercy does not become effective toward a man until justice has done its work. The just penalty for sin was exacted when Christ our Substitute died for us on the cross. However unpleasant this may sound to the ear of the natural man, it has ever been sweet to the ear of faith. Millions have been morally and spiritually transformed by this message, have lived lives of great moral power, and died at last peacefully trusting in it.

This message of justice discharged and mercy operative is more than a pleasant theological theory; it announces a fact made necessary by our deep human need. Because of our sin we are all under sentence of death, a judgement which resulted when justice confronted our moral situation. When infinite equity encountered our chronic and wilful in-equity, there was violent war between the two, a war which God won and must always win. But when the penitent sinner casts himself upon Christ for salvation, the moral situation is reversed. Justice confronts the changed situation and pronounces the believing man just. Thus justice actually goes over to the side of God's trusting children. This is the meaning of those daring words of the apostle John: 'If we confess our sins, he is faithful and just to forgive us our sins, and to cleanse us from all unrighteousness.'[7]

But God's justice stands for ever against the sinner in utter severity. The vague and tenuous hope that God is too kind to punish the ungodly has become a deadly opiate for the consciences of millions. It hushes their fears and allows them to practice all pleasant forms of iniquity while death draws every day nearer and the command to repent goes unregarded. As responsible moral beings we dare not so trifle with our eternal future.

Jesus, Thy blood and righteousness
My beauty are, my glorious dress;
'Midst flaming worlds, in these arrayed,
With joy shall I lift up my head.

Bold shall I stand in Thy great day;
For who aught to my charge shall lay?
Fully absolved through these I am –
From sin and fear, from guilt and shame.

Count N. L. von Zinzendorf

Notes

1 Gen. 18:25.
2 Ps. 97:2.

3 Ps. 94:1–3.
4 Dan. 9:7.
5 Rev. 15:3–4.
6 St Anselm, *op. cit.* p.14.
7 John 1:9.

18

The Mercy of God

Holy Father, Thy wisdom excites our admiration, Thy power fills us with fear, Thy omnipresence turns every spot of earth into holy ground; but how shall we thank Thee enough for Thy mercy which comes down to the lowest part of our need to give us beauty for ashes, the oil of joy for mourning, and for the spirit of heaviness a garment of praise? We bless and magnify Thy mercy, through Jesus Christ our Lord. Amen.

When through the blood of the everlasting covenant we children of the shadows reach at last our home in the light, we shall have a thousand strings to our harps, but the sweetest may well be the one tuned to sound forth most perfectly the mercy of God.

For what right will we have to be there? Did we not by our sins take part in that unholy rebellion which rashly sought to dethrone the glorious King of creation? And did we not in times past walk according to the course of this world, according to the evil prince of the power of the air, the spirit that now works in the sons of disobedience? And did we not all once live in the lusts of our flesh? And were we not by nature the children of wrath, even as others? But we who were one time enemies and alienated in our minds through wicked works shall then see God face to face and His name shall be in our foreheads. We who earned banishment shall enjoy communion; we who deserve the pains of hell shall know the bliss of heaven. And all through the tender mercy of our God, whereby the dayspring from on high hath visited us.

When all Thy mercies, O my God,
My rising soul surveys,
Transported with the view, I'm lost
In wonder, love, and praise.
Joseph Addison

Mercy is an attribute of God, an infinite and inexhaustible energy within the divine nature which disposes God to be actively compassionate. Both the Old and the New Testaments proclaim the mercy of God, but the Old has more than four times as much to say about it as the New.

We should banish from our minds for ever the common but erroneous notion that justice and judgement characterise the God of Israel, while mercy and grace belong to the Lord of the Church. Actually there is in principle no difference between the Old Testament and the New. In the New Testament Scriptures there is a fuller development of redemptive truth, but one God speaks in both dispensations, and what He speaks agrees with what He is. Wherever and whenever God appears to men, He acts like Himself. Whether in the Garden of Eden or the Garden of Gethsemane, God is merciful as well as just. He has always dealt in mercy with mankind and will always deal in justice when His mercy is despised. Thus He did in antediluvian times; thus when Christ walked among men; thus He is doing today and will continue always to do for no other reason than that He is God.

If we could remember that the divine mercy is not a temporary mood but an attribute of God's eternal being, we would no longer fear that it will some day cease to be. Mercy never began to be, but from eternity was; so it will never cease to be. It will never be more since it is in itself infinite; and it will never be less because the infinite cannot suffer diminution. Nothing that has occurred or will occur in heaven or earth or hell can change the tender mercies of our God. For ever His mercy stands, a boundless, overwhelming immensity of divine pity and compassion.

As judgement is God's justice confronting moral inequity, so mercy is the goodness of God confronting human suffering and guilt. Were there no guilt in the world, no pain and no tears, God would yet be infinitely merciful; but His mercy might well remain hidden in His heart, unknown to the created universe. No voice would be raised to celebrate the mercy of which none felt the need. It is human misery and sin that call forth the divine mercy.

'*Kyrie eleison! Christe eleison!*' the Church has pleaded through the centuries; but if I mistake not I hear in the voice of her pleading a note of sadness and despair. Her plaintive cry, so often repeated in that tone of resigned dejection, compels one to infer that she is praying for a boon she never actually expects to receive. She may go on dutifully to sing of the greatness of God and to recite the creed times beyond number, but her plea for mercy sounds like a forlorn hope and no more, as if mercy were a heavenly gift to be longed for but never really enjoyed.

Could our failure to capture the pure joy of mercy consciously experienced be the result of our unbelief or our ignorance, or both? It was so once in Israel. 'I bear them record,' Paul testified of Israel, 'that they have a zeal of God, but not according to knowledge.'[1] They failed because there was at least one thing they did not know, one thing that would have made the difference. And of Israel in the wilderness the Hebrew writer says, 'But the word preached did not profit them, not being mixed with faith in them that heard it.'[2] To receive mercy we must first know that God is merciful. And it is not enough to believe that He once showed mercy to Noah or Abraham or David and will again show mercy in some happy future day. We must believe that God's mercy is boundless, free and, through Jesus Christ our Lord, available to us now in our present situation.

We may plead for mercy for a lifetime in unbelief, and at the end of our days be still no more than sadly hopeful that we shall somewhere, sometime, receive it. This is to starve to death just outside the banquet hall into which we have been warmly invited. Or we may, if we will, lay hold on the mercy of God by faith, enter the hall, and sit down with the bold and avid souls who will not allow diffidence and unbelief to keep them from the feast of fat things prepared for them.

Arise, my soul, arise;
Shake off thy guilty fears;
The bleeding Sacrifice
In my behalf appears:
Before the throne my Surety stands,
My name is written on His hands.

My God is reconciled;
His pardoning voice I hear:
He owns me for His child;
I can no longer fear:
With confidence I now draw nigh,
And 'Father, Abba, Father,' cry.
Charles Wesley

Notes

1 Rom. 10:2.
2 Heb. 4:2.

19

The Grace of God

God of all grace, whose thoughts toward us are ever thoughts of peace and not of evil, give us hearts to believe that we are accepted in the Beloved; and give us minds to admire that perfection of moral wisdom which found a way to preserve the integrity of heaven and yet receive us there. We are astonished and marvel that one so holy and dread should invite us into Thy banqueting house and cause love to be the banner over us. We cannot express the gratitude we feel, but look Thou on our hearts and read it there. Amen.

In God mercy and grace are one; but as they reach us they are seen as two, related but not identical.

As mercy is God's goodness confronting human misery and guilt, so grace is His goodness directed toward human debt and demerit. It is by His grace that God imputes merit where none previously existed and declares no debt to be where one had been before.

Grace is the good pleasure of God that inclines Him to bestow benefits upon the undeserving. It is a self-existent principle inherent in the divine nature and appears to us as a self-caused propensity to pity the wretched, spare the guilty, welcome the outcast, and bring into favour those who were before under just disapprobation. Its use to us sinful men is to save us and make us sit together in heavenly places to demonstrate to the ages the exceeding riches of God's kindness to us in Christ Jesus.

We benefit eternally by God's being just what He is. Because He is what He is, He lifts up our heads out of the prison house, changes our prison garments for royal robes, and makes us to eat bread continually before Him all the days of our lives.

Grace takes its rise far back in the heart of God, in the awful and incomprehensible abyss of His holy being; but the channel through which it flows out to men is Jesus Christ, crucified and risen. The apostle Paul, who beyond all others is the exponent of grace in redemption, never disassociates God's grace from God's crucified Son. Always in his teachings the two are found together, organically one and inseparable.

A full and fair summation of Paul's teaching on this subject is found in his Epistle to the Ephesians: 'Having pre-destinated us unto the adoption of children by Jesus Christ to himself, according to the good pleasure of his will, to the praise of the glory of his grace, wherein he hath made us accepted in the beloved. In whom we have redemption through his blood, the forgiveness of sins, according to the riches of his grace.'[1]

John also, in the Gospel that bears his name, identifies Christ as the medium through which grace reaches mankind: 'For the law was given by Moses, but grace and truth came by Jesus Christ.'[2]

But right here it is easy to miss the path and go far astray from the truth; and some have done this. They have compelled this verse to stand by itself, unrelated to other scriptures bearing on the doctrine of grace, and have made it teach that Moses knew only law and Christ knows only grace. So the Old Testament is made to be a book of law and the New Testament a book of grace. The truth is quite otherwise.

The law was given to men through Moses, but it did not originate with Moses. It had existed in the heart of God from before the foundation of the world. On Mount Sinai it became the legal code for the nation of Israel; but the moral principles it embodies are eternal. There never was a time when the law did not represent the will of God for mankind nor a time when the violation of it did not bring its own penalty, though God was patient and sometimes 'winked' at wrongdoing because of the ignorance of the people. Paul's close-knit arguments in the third and fifth chapters of his epistle to the Romans make this very clear. The spring of Christian morality is the love of Christ, not the law of Moses; nevertheless there has been no abrogation of the principles of morality contained in the law. No privileged class exists exempt from that righteousness which the law enjoins.

The Old Testament is indeed a book of law, but not of law only. Before the great flood Noah 'found grace in the eyes of the Lord,'[3] and after the law was given God said to Moses, 'Thou hast found grace in my sight.'[4] And how could it be otherwise? God will always be Himself, and grace is an attribute of His holy being. He can no more hide His grace than the sun can hide its brightness. Men may flee from the sunlight to dark and musty caves of the earth, but they cannot put out the sun. So men may in any dispensation despise the grace of God, but they cannot extinguish it.

Had the Old Testament times been times of stern, unbending law alone the whole complexion of the early world would have been vastly less cheerful than we find it to be in the ancient writings. There could have been no Abraham, friend of God; no David, man after God's own heart; no Samuel, no Isaiah, no Daniel. The eleventh chapter of Hebrews, that Westminster Abbey of the spiritually great of the Old Testament, would stand dark and tenantless. Grace made sainthood possible in Old Testament days just as it does today.

No one was ever saved other than by grace, from Abel

to the present moment. Since mankind was banished from the eastward Garden, none has ever returned to the divine favour except through the sheer goodness of God. And wherever grace found any man it was always by Jesus Christ. Grace indeed came by Jesus Christ, but it did not wait for His birth in the manger or His death on the cross before it became operative. Christ is the Lamb slain from the foundation of the world. The first man in human history to be reinstated in the fellowship of God came through faith in Christ. In olden times men looked forward to Christ's redeeming work; in later times they gaze back upon it, but always they came and they come by grace, through faith.

We must keep in mind also that the grace of God is infinite and eternal. As it had no beginning, so it can have no end, and being an attribute of God, it is as boundless as infinitude.

Instead of straining to comprehend this as a theological truth, it would be better and simpler to compare God's grace with our need. We can never know the enormity of our sin, neither is it necessary that we should. What we can know is that 'where sin abounded, grace did much more abound'.[5]

To 'abound' in sin: that is the worst and the most we could or can do. The word *abound* defines the limit of our finite abilities; and although we feel our iniquities rise over us like a mountain, the mountain, nevertheless, has definable boundaries: it is so large, so high, it weighs only this certain amount and no more. But who shall define the limitless grace of God? Its 'much more' plunges our thoughts into infinitude and confounds them there. All thanks be to God for grace abounding.

We who feel ourselves alienated from the fellowship of God can now raise our discouraged heads and look up. Through the virtues of Christ's atoning death the cause of our banishment has been removed. We may return as the

Prodigal returned, and be welcome. As we approach the Garden, our home before the Fall, the flaming sword is withdrawn. The keepers of the tree of life stand aside when they see a son of grace approaching.

> Return, O wanderer, now return,
> And seek thy Father's face;
> Those new desires which in thee burn
> Were kindled by His grace.
>
> Return, O wanderer, now return,
> And wipe the falling tear:
> Thy Father calls, – no longer mourn;
> 'Tis love invites thee near.
>
> *William Benco Collyer*

Notes

1 Eph. 1:5–7.
2 John 1:17.
3 Gen. 6:8.
4 Ex. 33:17.
5 Rom. 5:20.

20

The Love of God

Our Father which art in heaven, we Thy children are often troubled in mind, hearing within us at once the affirmations of faith and the accusations of conscience. We are sure that there is in us nothing that could attract the love of One as holy and as just as Thou art. Yet Thou hast declared Thine unchanging love for us in Christ Jesus. If nothing in us can win Thy love, nothing in the universe can prevent Thee from loving us. Thy love is uncaused and undeserved. Thou art Thyself the reason for the love wherewith we are loved. Help us to believe the intensity, the eternity of the love that has found us. Then love will cast out fear; and our troubled hearts will be at peace, trusting not in what we are but in what Thou hast declared Thyself to be. Amen.

The apostle John, by the Spirit, wrote, 'God is love,'[1] and some have taken his words to be a definitive statement concerning the essential nature of God. This is a great error. John was by those words stating a fact, but he was not offering a definition.

Equating love with God is a major mistake which has produced much unsound religious philosophy and has brought forth a spate of vaporous poetry completely out of accord with the Holy Scriptures and altogether of another climate from that of historic Christianity.

Had the apostle declared that love is what God is, we

would be forced to infer that God is what love is. If literally God is love, then literally love is God, and we are in all duty bound to worship love as the only God there is. If love is equal to God then God is only equal to love, and God and love are identical. Thus we destroy the concept of personality in God and deny outright all His attributes save one, and that one we substitute for God. The God we have left is not the God of Israel; He is not the God and Father of our Lord Jesus Christ; He is not the God of the prophets and the apostles; He is not the God of the saints and reformers and martyrs, nor yet the God of the theologians and hymnists of the church.

For our souls' sake we must learn to understand the Scriptures. We must escape the slavery of words and give loyal adherence to meanings instead. Words should express ideas, not originate them. We say that God is love; we say that God is light; we say that Christ is truth; and we mean the words to be understood in much the same way that words are understood when we say of a man, 'He is kindness itself.' By so saying we are not stating that kindness and the man are identical, and no one understands our words in that sense.

The words 'God is love' mean that love is an essential attribute of God. Love is something true of God but it is not God. It expresses the way God is in His unitary being, as do the words holiness, justice, faithfulness and truth. Because God is immutable He always acts like Himself, and because He is a unity He never suspends one of His attributes in order to exercise another.

From God's other known attributes we may learn much about His love. We can know, for instance, that because God is self-existent, His love had no beginning; because He is eternal, His love can have no end; because He is infinite, it has no limit; because He is holy, it is the quintessence of all spotless purity; because He is immense, His love is an incomprehensibly vast, bottomless, shoreless sea before which we kneel in joyful silence and from which the loftiest eloquence retreats confused and abashed.

Yet if we would know God and for other's sake tell what we know, we must try to speak of His love. All Christians have tried, but none has ever done it very well. I can no more do justice to that awesome and wonder-filled theme than a child can grasp a star. Still, by reaching toward the star the child may call attention to it and even indicate the direction one must look to see it. So, as I stretch my heart toward the high, shining love of God, someone who has not before known about it may be encouraged to look up and have hope.

We do not know, and we may never know, what love *is*, but we can know how it manifests itself, and that is enough for us here. First we see it showing itself as good will. Love wills the good of all and never wills harm or evil to any. This explains the words of the apostle John: 'There is no fear in love; but perfect love casteth out fear.'[2] Fear is the painful emotion that arises at the thought that we may be harmed or made to suffer. This fear persists while we are subject to the will of someone who does not desire our well-being. The moment we come under the protection of one of good will, fear is cast out. A child lost in a crowded store is full of fear because it sees the strangers around it as enemies. In its mother's arms a moment later all the terror subsides. The known good will of the mother casts out fear.

The world is full of enemies, and as long as we are subject to the possibility of harm from these enemies, fear is inevitable. The effort to conquer fear without removing the causes is altogether futile. The heart is wiser than the apostles of tranquillity. As long as we are in the hands of chance, as long as we must look for hope to the law of averages, as long as we must trust for survival to our ability to outthink or outmanoeuvre the enemy, we have every good reason to be afraid. And fear hath torment.

To know that love is of God and to enter into the secret place leaning upon the arm of the Beloved – this and only this can cast out fear. Let a man become convinced that nothing can harm him and instantly for him all fear goes out of the universe. The nervous reflex, the natural revulsion to physical pain may be felt sometimes, but the deep torment of fear is gone for ever. God is love and God is sovereign. His love disposes Him to desire our everlasting welfare and His sovereignty enables Him to secure it. Nothing can hurt a good man.

> The body they may kill;
> God's truth abideth still,
> His kingdom is for ever.
> *Martin Luther*

God's love tells us that He is friendly and His Word assures us that He is our friend and wants us to be His friends. No man with a trace of humility would first think that he is a friend of God; but the idea did not originate with men. Abraham would never have said, 'I am God's friend,' but God Himself said that Abraham was His friend. The disciples might well have hesitated to claim friendship with Christ, but Christ said to them, 'Ye are my friends.'[3] Modesty may demur at so rash a thought, but audacious faith dares to believe the Word and claim friendship with God. We do God more honour by believing what He has said about Himself and having the courage to come boldly to the throne of grace than by hiding in self-conscious humility among the trees of the garden.

Love is also an emotional identification. It considers nothing its own but gives all freely to the object of its affection. We see this constantly in our world of men and women. A young mother, thin and tired, nurses at her breast a plump and healthy baby, and far from complaining, the mother gazes down at her child with eyes shining with happiness and pride. Acts of self-sacrifice are common to love. Christ said of Himself, 'Greater love hath no man than this, that a man lay down his life for his friends.'[4]

It is a strange and beautiful eccentricity of the free God that He has allowed His heart to be emotionally identified with men. Self-sufficient as He is, He wants our love and will not be satisfied till He gets it. Free as He is, He has let His heart be bound to us for ever.

> Herein is love, not that we loved God, but that he loved us, and sent his Son to be the propitiation for our sins.[5]

'For our soul is so specially loved of Him that is highest,' says Julian of Norwich, 'that it overpasseth the knowing of all creatures: that is to say, there is no creature that is made that may know how much and how sweetly and how tenderly our Maker loveth us. And therefore we may with grace and His help stand in spiritual beholding, with everlasting marvel of this high, overpassing, inestimable love that Almighty God hath to us of His goodness.'[6]

Another characteristic of love is that it takes pleasure in its object. God enjoys His creation. The apostle John says frankly that God's purpose in creation was His own pleasure. God is happy in His love for all that He has made. We cannot miss the feeling of pleasure in God's delighted references to His handiwork. Psalm 104 is a divinely inspired nature poem almost rhapsodic in its happiness, and the delight of God is felt throughout it. 'The glory of the Lord shall endure for ever: the Lord shall rejoice in his works.'[7]

The Lord takes peculiar pleasure in His saints. Many think of God as far removed, gloomy and mightily displeased with everything, gazing down in a mood of fixed apathy upon a world in which He has long ago lost interest;

but this is to think erroneously. True, God hates sin and can never look with pleasure upon iniquity, but where men seek to do God's will He responds in genuine affection. Christ in His atonement has removed the bar to the divine fellowship. Now in Christ all believing souls are objects of God's delight.

> The Lord thy God in the midst of thee is mighty; he will save, he will rejoice over thee with joy; he will rest in his love, he will joy over thee with singing.[8]

According to the book of Job, God's work of creation was done to musical accompaniment. 'Where wast thou,' God asks, 'when I laid the foundations of the earth... when the morning stars sang together, and all the sons of God shouted for joy?'[9] John Dryden carried the idea a bit further than this, but not, perhaps, too far to be true:

> From harmony, from heavenly harmony,
> This universal frame began:
> When nature underneath a heap
> Of jarring atoms lay,
> And could not heave her head,
> The tuneful voice was heard from high,
> 'Arise, ye more than dead!'
> Then cold, and hot, and moist, and dry,
> In order to their stations leap,
> And Music's power obey.
> From harmony, from heavenly harmony,
> This universal frame began:
> From harmony to harmony
> Through all the compass of the notes it ran,
> The diapason closing full in Man.
> *From* 'A Song for St Cecilia's Day'

Music is both an expression and a source of pleasure, and the pleasure that is purest and nearest to God is the pleasure of love. Hell is a place of no pleasure because there is no love there. Heaven is full of music because it is the place where the pleasures of holy love abound. Earth is the place where the pleasures of love are mixed with pain, for sin is here, and hate and ill will. In such a world as ours love must sometimes suffer, as Christ suffered in giving Himself for His own. But we have the certain promise that the causes of sorrow will finally be abolished and the new race enjoy for ever a world of selfless, perfect love.

It is of the nature of love that it cannot lie quiescent. It is active, creative, and benign. 'God commendeth his love toward us, in that, while we were yet sinners, Christ died for us.'[10] 'God so loved the world, that he gave his only begotten Son.'[11] So it must be where love is; love must ever give to its own, whatever the cost. The apostles rebuked the young churches sharply because a few of their members had forgotten this and had allowed their love to spend itself in personal enjoyment while their brethren were in need. 'But whoso hath this world's good, and seeth his brother have need, and shutteth up his bowels of compassion from him, how dwelleth the love of God in him?'[12] So wrote that John who has been known to the centuries as 'the Beloved'.

The love of God is one of the great realities of the universe, a pillar upon which the hope of the world rests. But it is a personal, intimate thing, too. God does not love populations, He loves people. He loves not masses, but men. He loves us all with a mighty love that has no beginning and can have no end.

In Christian experience there is a highly satisfying love content that distinguishes it from all other religions and elevates it to heights far beyond even the purest and noblest philosophy. This love content is more than a thing; it is God Himself in the midst of His Church singing over His people. True Christian joy is the heart's harmonious response to the Lord's song of love.

Thou hidden love of God, whose height,
  Whose depth unfathomed, no man knows,
I see from far Thy beauteous light,
  Inly I sigh for Thy repose;
My heart is pained, nor can it be
At rest till it finds rest in Thee.

Gerhard Tersteegen

Notes

1 1 John 4:8.
2 1 John 4:18.
3 John 15:14.
4 John 15:13.
5 1 John 4:10.
6 Julian of Norwich, *op. cit.* p.58.
7 Ps. 104:31.
8 Zeph. 3:17.
9 Job 38:4, 7.
10 Rom. 5:8.
11 John 3:16.
12 1 John 3:17.

21

The Holiness of God

Glory be to God on high. We praise Thee, we bless Thee, we worship Thee, for Thy great glory. Lord, I uttered that I understood not; things too wonderful for me which I knew not. I heard of Thee by the hearing of the ear, but now mine eye seeth Thee and I abhor myself in dust and ashes. O Lord, I will lay my hand upon my mouth. Once have I spoken, yea, twice, but I will proceed no further.

But while I was musing the fire burned. Lord, I must speak of Thee, lest by my silence I offend against the generation of Thy children. Behold, Thou hast chosen the foolish things of the world to confound the wise, and the weak things of the world to confound the mighty. O Lord, forsake me not. Let me show forth Thy strength unto this generation and Thy power to everyone that is to come. Raise up prophets and seers in Thy Church who shall magnify Thy glory and through Thine almighty Spirit restore to Thy people the knowledge of the holy. Amen.

The moral shock suffered by us through our mighty break with the high will of heaven has left us all with a permanent trauma affecting every part of our nature. There is disease both in ourselves and in our environment.

The sudden realisation of his personal depravity came like a stroke from heaven upon the trembling heart of Isaiah at the moment when he had his revolutionary vision of the holiness of God. His pain-filled cry, 'Woe is me! for

I am undone; because I am a man of unclean lips, and I dwell in the midst of a people of unclean lips: for mine eyes have seen the King, the Lord of hosts,"[1] expresses the feeling of every man who has discovered himself under his disguises and has been confronted with an inward sight of the holy whiteness that is God. Such an experience cannot but be emotionally violent.

Until we have seen ourselves as God sees us, we are not likely to be much disturbed over conditions around us as long as they do not get so far out of hand as to threaten our comfortable way of life. We have learned to live with unholiness and have come to look upon it as the natural and expected thing. We are not disappointed that we do not find all truth in our teachers or faithfulness in our politicians or complete honesty in our merchants or full trustworthiness in our friends. That we may continue to exist we make such laws as are necessary to protect us from our fellow men and let it go at that.

Neither the writer nor the reader of these words is qualified to appreciate the holiness of God. Quite literally a new channel must be cut through the desert of our minds to allow the sweet waters of truth that will heal our great sickness to flow in. We cannot grasp the true meaning of the divine holiness by thinking of someone or something very pure and then raising the concept to the highest degree we are capable of. God's holiness is not simply the best we know infinitely bettered. We know nothing like the divine holiness. It stands apart, unique, unapproachable, incomprehensible and unattainable. The natural man is blind to it. He may fear God's power and admire His wisdom, but His holiness he cannot even imagine.

Only the Spirit of the Holy One can impart to the human spirit the knowledge of the holy. Yet as electric power flows only through a conductor, so the Spirit flows through truth and must find some measure of truth in the mind before He can illuminate the heart. Faith wakes at the voice of truth but responds to no other sound. 'Faith cometh by hearing, and hearing by the word of God.'[2] Theological knowledge is the medium through which the Spirit flows into the human heart, yet there must be humble penitence in the heart before truth can produce faith. The Spirit of God is the Spirit of truth. It is possible to have some truth in the mind without having the Spirit in the heart, but it is never possible to have the Spirit apart from truth.

In his penetrating study of the holy, Rudolf Otto makes a strong case for the presence in the human mind of something he names the 'numinous,' by which, apparently, he means a sense that there is in the world a vague, incomprehensible Something, the *Mysterium Tremendum*, the awesome *mystery*, surrounding and enfolding the universe. This is an *it*, an awful *thing*, and can never be intellectually conceived, only sensed and felt in the depths of the human spirit. It remains as a permanent religious instinct, a feeling for that unnamed, undiscoverable *presence* that 'runs quicksilverlike through creation's veins' and sometimes stuns the mind by confronting it with a supernatural, suprarational manifestation of itself. The man thus confronted is brought down and overwhelmed and can only tremble and be silent.

This nonrational dread, this feeling for the uncreated *mystery* in the world, is behind all religion. The pure religion of the Bible, no less than the basest animism of the naked tribesman, exists only because this basic instinct is present in human nature. Of course, the difference between the religion of an Isaiah or a Paul and that of the animist is that one has truth and the other has not; he has only the 'numinous' instinct. He 'feels after' an unknown God, but an Isaiah and a Paul have found the true God through His own self-disclosure in the inspired Scriptures.

The feeling for mystery, even for the *Great Mystery*, is

basic in human nature and indispensable to religious faith, but it is not enough. Because of it men may whisper, 'That awful *thing*,' but they do not cry, 'Mine Holy One!'[3] In the Hebrew and Christian Scriptures God carries forward His self-revelation and gives it personality and moral content. This awful *presence* is shown to be not a *thing* but a moral *being* with all the warm qualities of genuine personality. more than this, He is the absolute quintessence of moral excellence, infinitely perfect in righteousness, purity, rectitude, and incomprehensible holiness. And in all this He is uncreated, self-sufficient and beyond the power of human thought to conceive or human speech to utter.

Through the self-revelation of God in the Scriptures and the illumination of the Holy Spirit the Christian gains everything and loses nothing. To his idea of God there are added the twin concepts of personality and moral character, but there remains the original sense of wonder and fear in the presence of the world-filling *mystery*. Today his heart may leap up with the happy cry, 'Abba Father, my Lord and my God!' Tomorrow he may kneel with delighted trembling to admire and adore the high and lofty One that inhabiteth eternity.

Holy is the way God is. To be holy He does not conform to a standard. He is that standard. He is absolutely holy with an infinite, incomprehensible fullness of purity that is incapable of being other than it is. Because He is holy, all His attributes are holy; that is, whatever we think of as belonging to God must be thought of as holy.

God is holy and He has made holiness the moral condition necessary to the health of His universe. Sin's temporary presence in the world only accents this. Whatever is holy is healthy; evil is a moral sickness that must end ultimately in death. The formation of the language itself suggests this, the English word *holy* deriving from the Anglo-Saxon *halig, hal,* meaning 'well, whole.'

Since God's first concern for His universe is its moral

health, that is, its holiness, whatever is contrary to this is necessarily under His eternal displeasure. To preserve His creation God must destroy whatever would destroy it. When He arises to put down iniquity and save the world from irreparable moral collapse, He is said to be angry. Every wrathful judgement in the history of the world has been a holy act of preservation. The holiness of God, the wrath of God, and the health of the creation are inseparably united. God's wrath is His utter intolerance of whatever degrades and destroys. He hates iniquity as a mother hates the polio that would take the life of her child.

God is holy with an absolute holiness that knows no degrees, and this He cannot impart to His creatures. But there is a relative and contingent holiness which He shares with angels and seraphim in heaven and with redeemed men on earth as their preparation for heaven. This holiness God can and does impart to His children. He shares it with them by imputation and by impartation, and because He has made it available to them through the blood of the Lamb, He requires it of them. To Israel first and later to His Church God spoke, saying, 'Be ye holy; for I am holy.'[4] He did not say 'Be ye as holy as I am holy,' for that would be to demand of us absolute holiness, something that belongs to God alone. Before the uncreated fire of God's holiness angels veil their faces. Yea, the heavens are not clean, and the stars are not pure in His sight. No honest man can say, 'I am holy,' but neither is any honest man willing to ignore the solemn words of the inspired writer, 'Follow peace with all men and holiness, without which no man shall see the Lord.'[5]

Caught in this dilemma, what are we Christians to do? We must like Moses cover ourselves with faith and humility while we steal a quick look at the God whom no man can see and live. The broken and the contrite heart He will not despise. We must hide our unholiness in the wounds of Christ as Moses hid himself in the cleft of the rock while the glory of God passed by. We must take refuge from God in God. Above all we must believe that God sees us perfect in His Son while He disciplines and chastens and purges us that we may be partakers of His holiness.

By faith and obedience, by constant meditation on the holiness of God, by loving righteousness and hating iniquity, by a growing acquaintance with the Spirit of holiness, we can acclimate ourselves to the fellowship of the saints on earth and prepare ourselves for the eternal companionship of God and the saints above. Thus, as they say when humble believers meet, we will have a heaven to go to heaven in.

How dread are Thine eternal years,
O everlasting Lord!
By prostrate spirits day and night
Incessantly adored!

How beautiful, how beautiful
The sight of Thee must be,
Thine endless wisdom, boundless power,
And awful purity!

Oh how I fear Thee, living God!
With deepest, tenderest fears,
And worship Thee with trembling hope,
And penitential tears.

Frederick W. Faber

Notes

1 Isa. 6:5.
2 Rom. 10:17.
3 Hab. 1:12.
4 1 Pet. 1:16.
5 Heb. 12:14.

22

The Sovereignty of God

Who wouldst not fear Thee, O Lord God of hosts, most high and most terrible? For Thou art Lord alone. Thou hast made heaven and the heaven of heavens, the earth and all things that are therein, and in Thy hand is the soul of every living thing. Thou sittest king upon the flood; yea, Thou sittest King for ever. Thou art a great King over all the earth. Thou art clothed with strength; honour and majesty are before Thee. Amen.

God's sovereignty is the attribute by which He rules His entire creation, and to be sovereign God must be all-knowing, all-powerful, and absolutely free. The reasons are these:

Were there even one datum of knowledge, however small, unknown to God, His rule would break down at that point. To be Lord over all the creation, He must possess all knowledge. And were God lacking one infinitesimal modicum of power, that lack would end His reign and undo His kingdom; that one stray atom of power would belong to someone else and God would be a limited ruler and hence not sovereign.

Furthermore, His sovereignty requires that He be absolutely free, which means simply that He must be free to do whatever He wills to do anywhere at any time to carry out His eternal purpose in every single detail without interference. Were He less than free He must be less than sovereign.

To grasp the idea of unqualified freedom requires a vigorous effort of the mind. We are not psychologically conditioned to understand freedom except in its imperfect forms. Our concepts of it have been shaped in a world where no absolute freedom exists. Here each natural object is dependent upon many other objects, and that dependence limits its freedom.

Wordsworth at the beginning of his 'Prelude' rejoiced that he had escaped the city where he had long been pent up and was 'now free, free as a bird to settle where I will'. But to be free as a bird is not to be free at all. The naturalist knows that the supposedly free bird actually lives its entire life in a cage made of fears, hungers, and instincts; it is limited by weather conditions, varying air pressures, the local food supply, predatory beasts, and that strangest of all bonds, the irresistible compulsion to stay within the small plot of land and air assigned it by birdland comity. The freest bird is, along with every other created thing, held in constant check by a net of necessity. Only God is free.

God is said to be absolutely free because no one and no thing can hinder Him or compel Him or stop Him. He is able to do as He pleases always, everywhere, for ever. To be thus free means also that He must possess universal authority. That He has unlimited power we know from the Scriptures and may deduce from certain other of His attributes. But what about His authority?

Even to discuss the authority of Almighty God seems a bit meaningless, and to question it would be absurd. Can we imagine the Lord God of hosts having to request permission of anyone or to apply for anything to a higher body? To whom would God go for permission? Who is higher than the Highest? Who is mightier than the Almighty? Whose position antedates that of the Eternal?

At whose throne would God kneel? Where is the greater one to whom He must appeal? 'Thus saith the Lord the King of Israel, and his redeemer the Lord of hosts; I am the first, and I am the last; and beside me there is no God.'[1]

The sovereignty of God is a fact well established in the Scriptures and declared aloud by the logic of truth. But admittedly it raises certain problems which have not to this time been satisfactorily solved. These are mainly two.

The first is the presence in the creation of those things which God cannot approve, such as evil, pain, and death. If God is sovereign He could have prevented their coming into existence. Why did He not do so?

The *Zend-Ayesta*, sacred book of Zoroastrianism, loftiest of the great non-biblical religions, got around this difficulty neatly enough by postulating a theological dualism. There were two gods, Ormazd and Ahriman, and these between them created the world. The good Ormazd made all good things and the evil Ahriman made the rest. It was quite simple. Ormazd had no sovereignty to worry about, and apparently did not mind sharing his prerogatives with another.

For the Christian this explanation will not do, for it flatly contradicts the truth taught so emphatically throughout the whole Bible, that there is one God and that He alone created the heaven and the earth and all the things that are therein. God's attributes are such as to make impossible the existence of another god. The Christian admits that he does not have the final answer to the riddle of permitted evil. But he knows what that answer is not. And he knows that the *Zend-Avesta* does not have it either.

While a complete explanation of the origin of sin eludes us, there are a few things we do know. In His sovereign wisdom God has permitted evil to exist in carefully restricted areas of His creation, a kind of fugitive outlaw whose activities are temporary and limited in scope. In doing this God has acted according to His infinite wisdom and goodness. More than that no one knows at present; and more than that no one needs to know. The name of God is sufficient guarantee of the perfection of His works.

Another real problem created by the doctrine of the divine sovereignty has to do with the will of man. If God rules His universe by His sovereign decrees, how is it possible for man to exercise free choice? And if he cannot exercise freedom of choice, how can he be held responsible for his conduct? Is he not a mere puppet whose actions are determined by a behind-the-scenes God who pulls the strings as it pleases Him?

The attempt to answer these questions has divided the Christian church neatly into two camps which have borne the names of two distinguished theologians, Jacobus Arminius and John Calvin. Most Christians are content to get into one camp or the other and deny either sovereignty to God or free will to man. It appears possible, however, to reconcile these two positions without doing violence to either, although the effort that follows may prove deficient to partisans of one camp or the other.

Here is my view: God sovereignly decreed that man should be free to exercise moral choice, and man from the beginning has fulfilled that decree by making his choice between good and evil. When he chooses to do evil, he does not thereby countervail the sovereign will of God but fulfills it, inasmuch as the eternal decree decided not which choice the man should make but that he should be free to make it. If in His absolute freedom God has willed to give man limited freedom, who is there to stay His hand or say, 'What doest thou?'[2] Man's will is free because God is sovereign. A God less than sovereign could not bestow moral freedom upon His creatures. He would be afraid to do so.

Perhaps a homely illustration might help us to understand. An ocean liner leaves New York bound for Liverpool. Its destination has been determined by proper authorities. Nothing can change it. This is at least a faint picture of sovereignty.

On the board the liner are several scores of passengers. These are not in chains, neither are their activities determined for them by decree. They are completely free to move about as they will. They eat, sleep, play, lounge about on the deck, read, talk, altogether as they please; but all the while the great liner is carrying them steadily onward toward a predetermined port.

Both freedom and sovereignty are present here and they do not contradict each other. So it is, I believe, with man's freedom and the sovereignty of God. The mighty liner of God's sovereign design keeps its steady course over the sea of history. God moves undisturbed and unhindered toward the fulfilment of those eternal purposes which He purposed in Christ Jesus before the world began. We do not know all that is included in those purposes, but enough has been disclosed to furnish us with a broad outline of things to come and to give us good hope and firm assurance of future well-being.

We know that God will fulfill every promise made to the prophets; we know that sinners will some day be cleansed out of the earth; we know that a ransomed company will enter into the joy of God and that the righteous will shine forth in the kingdom of their Father; we know that God's perfections will yet receive universal acclamation, that all created intelligences will own Jesus Christ Lord to the glory of God the Father, that the present imperfect order will be done away, and a new heaven and a new earth will be established for ever.

Toward all this God is moving with infinite wisdom and perfect precision of action. No one can dissuade Him from His purposes; nothing turn Him aside from His plans. Since He is omniscient, there can be no unforeseen circumstances, no accidents. As He is sovereign, there can be no countermanded orders, no breakdown in authority; and as He is omnipotent, there can be no want of power to achieve His chosen ends. God is sufficient unto Himself for all these things.

In the meanwhile things are not as smooth as this quick outline might suggest. The mystery of iniquity doth already work. Within the broad field of God's sovereign, permissive will the deadly conflict of good with evil continues with increasing fury. God will yet have His way in the whirlwind and the storm, but the storm and the whirlwind are here, and as responsible beings we must make our choice in the present moral situation.

Certain things have been decreed by the free determination of God, and one of these is the law of choice and consequences. God has decreed that all who willingly commit themselves to His Son Jesus Christ in the obedience of faith shall receive eternal life and become sons of God. He has also decreed that all who love darkness and continue in rebellion against the high authority of heaven shall remain in a state of spiritual alienation and suffer eternal death at last.

Reducing the whole matter to individual terms, we arrive at some vital and highly personal conclusions. In the moral conflict now raging around us whoever is on God's side is on the winning side and cannot lose; whoever is on the other side is on the losing side and cannot win. Here there is no chance, no gamble. There is freedom to choose which side we shall be on but no freedom to negotiate the results of the choice once it is made. By the mercy of God we may repent a wrong choice and alter the consequences by making a new and right choice. Beyond that we cannot go.

The whole matter of moral choice centres around Jesus Christ. Christ stated it plainly: 'He that is not with me is against me,'[3] and, 'No man cometh unto the Father, but by me.'[4] The gospel message embodies three distinct elements: an announcement, a command, and a call. It announces the good news of redemption accomplished in mercy; it commands all men everywhere to repent and it calls all men to surrender to the terms of grace by believing on Jesus Christ as Lord and Saviour.

We must all choose whether we will obey the gospel or turn away in unbelief and reject its authority. Our choice is our own, but the consequences of the choice have already been determined by the sovereign will of God, and from this there is no appeal.

The Lord descended from above,
  And bowed the heavens most high,
And underneath His feet He cast
  The darkness of the sky.

On cherubim and seraphim
  Full royally He rode,
And on the wings of mighty winds
  Came flying all abroad.

He sat serene upon the floods,
  Their fury to restrain;
And He, as sovereign Lord and King,
  For evermore shall reign.
Psalm paraphrase, by Thomas Sternhold

Notes

1 Isa. 44:6.
2 Dan. 4:35.
3 Matt. 12:30.
4 John 14:6.

23

The Open Secret

When viewed from the perspective of eternity, the most critical need of this hour may well be that the Church should be brought back from her long Babylonian captivity and the name of God be glorified in her again as of old. Yet we must not think of the Church as an anonymous body, a mystical religious abstraction. We Christians are the Church and whatever we do is what the Church is doing. The matter, therefore, is for each of us a personal one. Any forward step in the Church must begin with the individual.

What can we plain Christians do to bring back the departed glory? Is there some secret we may learn? Is there a formula for personal revival we can apply to the present situation, to our own situation? The answer to these questions is *yes*.

Yet the answer may easily disappoint some persons, for it is anything but profound. I bring no esoteric cryptogram, no mystic code to be painfully deciphered. I appeal to no hidden law of the unconscious, no occult knowledge meant only for the few. The secret is an open one which the wayfaring man may read. It is simply the old and ever-new counsel: *Acquaint thyself with God*. To regain her lost power the Church must see heaven opened and have a transforming vision of God.

But the God we must see is not the utilitarian God who is having such a run of popularity today, whose chief claim to men's attention is His ability to bring them success in their various undertakings and who for that reason is being cajoled and flattered by everyone who wants a favour. The God we must learn to know is the Majesty in the heavens, God the Father Almighty, Maker of heaven and earth, the only wise God our Saviour. He it is that sitteth upon the circle of the earth, who stretcheth out the heavens as a curtain and spreadeth them out as a tent to dwell in, who bringeth out His starry host by number and calleth them all by name through the greatness of His power, who seeth the works of man as vanity, who putteth no confidence in princes and asks no counsel of kings.

Knowledge of such a being cannot be gained by study alone. It comes by a wisdom the natural man knows nothing of, neither can know, because it is spiritually discerned. To know God is at once the easiest and the most difficult thing in the world. It is easy because the knowledge is not won by hard mental toil, but is something freely given. As sunlight falls free on the open field, so the knowledge of the holy God is a free gift to men who are open to receive it. But this knowledge is difficult because there are conditions to be met and the obstinate nature of fallen man does not take kindly to them.

Let me present a brief summary of these conditions as taught by the Bible and repeated through the centuries by the holiest, sweetest saints the world has ever known:

First, we must forsake our sins. The belief that a holy God cannot be known by men of confirmed evil lives is not new to the Christian religion. The Hebrew book, *The Wisdom of Solomon*, which antedates Christianity by many years, has the following passage:

> Love righteousness, ye that be judges of the earth: think of the Lord with a good heart, and in simplicity of heart seek

> him. For he will be found of them that tempt him not; and showeth himself unto such as do not distrust him. For froward thoughts separate from God: and his power, when it is tried, reproveth the unwise. For unto a malicious soul wisdom shall not enter; nor dwell in the body that is subject to sin. For the holy spirit of discipline will flee deceit, and remove from thoughts that are without understanding, and will not abide when unrighteousness cometh in.

This same thought is found in various sayings throughout the inspired Scriptures, the best known probably being the words of Christ, 'Blessed are the pure in heart: for they shall see God.'[1]

Second, there must be an utter committal of the whole life to Christ in faith. This is what it means to 'believe in Christ'. It involves a volitional and emotional attachment to Him accompanied by a firm purpose to obey Him in all things. This requires that we keep His commandments, carry our cross, and love God and our fellow men.

Third, there must be a reckoning of ourselves to have died unto sin and to be alive unto God in Christ Jesus, followed by a throwing open of the entire personality to the inflow of the Holy Spirit. Then we must practise whatever self-discipline is required to walk in the Spirit, and trample under our feet the lusts of the flesh.

Fourth, we must boldly repudiate the cheap values of the fallen world and become completely detached in spirit from everything that unbelieving men set their hearts upon, allowing ourselves only the simplest enjoyments of nature which God has bestowed alike upon the just and the unjust.

Fifth, we must practise the art of long and loving meditation upon the majesty of God. This will take some effort, for the concept of majesty has all but disappeared from the human race. The focal point of man's interest is now himself. Humanism in its various forms has displaced theology as the key to the understanding of life. When the nineteenth-century poet Swinburne wrote, 'Glory to man in the highest! for man is the master of things,' he gave to the modern world its new Te Deum. All this must be reversed by a deliberate act of the will and kept so by a patient effort of the mind.

God is a person and can be known in increasing degrees of intimate acquaintance as we prepare our hearts for the wonder. It may be necessary for us to alter our former beliefs about God as the glory that gilds the sacred Scriptures dawns over our interior lives. We may also need to break quietly and graciously with the lifeless textualism that prevails among the gospel churches, and to protest the frivolous character of much that passes for Christianity among us. By this we may for the time lose friends and gain a passing reputation for being holier-than-thou; but no man who permits the expectation of unpleasant consequences to influence him in a matter like this is fit for the kingdom of God.

Sixth, as the knowledge of God becomes more wonderful, greater service to our fellow men will become for us imperative. This blessed knowledge is not given to be enjoyed selfishly. The more perfectly we know God the more we will feel the desire to translate the new-found knowledge into deeds of mercy toward suffering humanity. The God who gave all to us will continue to give all *through* us as we come to know Him better.

Thus far we have considered the individual's personal relation to God, but like the ointment of a man's right hand, which by its fragrance 'betrayeth itself', any intensified knowledge of God will soon begin to affect those around us in the Christian community. And we must seek purposefully to share our increasing light with the fellow members of the household of God.

This we can best do by keeping the majesty of God in full focus in all our public services. Not only our private prayers should be filled with God, but our witnessing, our singing, our preaching, our writing should centre around the person of our holy, holy Lord and extol continually the greatness of His dignity and power. There is a glorified man on the right hand of the Majesty in heaven faithfully representing us there. We are left for a season among men; let us faithfully represent Him here.

The Set of the Sail

by A. W. Tozer

In characteristic style Tozer helps us to raise our sights by pointing us to God's eternal plan for our lives. As timely now as when they were first written, these chapters remind us of the blessings promised to those in Christ. Avoiding the pitfalls along the way, we can press on to the maturity God desires for all his children.

'Men and women of the Bible who have left us a record of spiritual greatness born out of a will firmly set to do the will of God . . . did not try to float to heaven on a perfumed cloud, but cheerfully accepted the fact that "with purpose of heart they must cleave to the Lord".

'Let us, then, set our sails in the will of God. If we do this we will certainly find ourselves moving in the right direction, no matter which way the wind blows.'

A. W. Tozer

A joint publication

STL Books and Kingsway Publications

Faith Beyond Reason

by A. W. Tozer

A. W. Tozer earned the reputation of 'twentieth century prophet', for he had a close walk with God and recognised the real issues at stake among evangelical Christians.

Here *faith* is the primary issue; Dr Tozer insists upon a faith that soars beyond reason to rest upon the character of God. Other areas covered include the *conscience*, the *transformed nature*, *usefulness in service* and the *second coming of Christ*.

A joint publication

STL Books and Kingsway Publications

Whatever Happened to Worship?

by A. W. Tozer

This is the book A. W. Tozer intended to write next. Now, more than twenty years after he was called home to heaven, it is available—compiled from tapes of sermons preached to his congregations in Toronto.

'True worship,' says Tozer, 'is to be so personally and hopelessly in love with God, that the idea of a transfer of affection never even remotely exists.'

A joint publication

STL Books and Kingsway Publications

The Divine Conquest

by A. W. Tozer

'The essentiality of a right interior life was the burden of Christ's teaching, and was without doubt one of the main causes of His rejection of those notorious externalists, the Pharisees. Paul also preached continually the doctrine of the indwelling Christ, and history will reveal that the Church has gained or lost power exactly as she has moved toward or away from the inwardness of her faith.'

(from the author's Preface)

In a day when there are so many confusing currents in the church, Dr Tozer points the way forward to inner spiritual reality and power.

A joint publication

STL Books and Kingsway Publications K

Leaning into the Wind

by A. W. Tozer

What is the way ahead for the church? What does renewal really involve? Are we ready for revival?

These and other related issues are dealt with uncompromisingly by Dr Tozer in this volume. According to Tozer, Christians must choose between easy conversions – or saintliness; entrenchment – or trust in the Spirit; big business methods – or New Testament principles; compromise – or a strong resolve to follow God even though it takes all our strength to resist other forces and 'lean into the wind'.

'Here are . . . words to wound but not destroy, designed as a clarion call for God's people to return to long forsaken positions in order to regain the ground that has been so easily lost.'
Clive Calver.

A joint publication

STL Books and Kingsway Publications K

The Pursuit of God

by A. W. Tozer

'This book is a modest attempt to aid God's hungry children so to find Him. Nothing here is new except in the sense that it is a discovery which my own heart has made of spiritual realities most delightful and wonderful to me. Others before me have gone much farther into these holy mysteries than I have done, but if my fire is not large it is yet real, and there may be those who can light their candle at its flame.'

(from the author's Preface)

A joint publication

STL Books and Kingsway Publications